KORETOSHI MARUYAMA

Aikido with Ki

Supervised by KOICHI TOHEI

KI NO KENKYUKAI H.Q.

Published by KI NO KENKYUKAI H.Q., Tokyo, Japan.

Distributors:
UNITED STATES: *Kodansha International/USA, Ltd., through Harper & Row, Publishers, Inc., 10 East 53rd Street, New York, N.Y. 10022.* SOUTH AMERICA: *Harper & Row, Publishers, Inc., International Department.* CANADA: *Fitzhenry & Whiteside Ltd., 150 Lesmill Road, Don Mills, Ontario M3B 2T6, Mexco and Central America : HARLS S.A. de C.V., Apartado 30-546, Mexico 4,D.F.* BRITISH ISLES: *International Book Distributors Ltd., 66 Wood Lane End, Hemel Hempstead, Herts HP2 4RG.* EUROPEAN CONTINENT: *Fleetbooks, S.A. c/o Feffer & Simons (Nederland) B.V., Rijnkade, 170 Weesp, The Netherlands.* AUSTRALIA AND NEW ZEALAND: *Book Wise (Australia) Pty, Ltd., 1 Jeanes Street, Beverley, South Australia 5009.* THE FAR EAST AND JAPAN: *Japan Publication Trading Co., Ltd., 1–2–1, Sarugaku-cho, Chiyoda-ku,. Tokyo 101.*

First edition: March 1984

ISBN 0-87040-566-7

Printed in Japan

KOICHI TOHEI

INTRODUCTION

The founder of Aikido, Morihei Ueshiba, was my Master. He was born in 1885 and practised many martial arts from the time of his boyhood. Finally he learned Daitoryu-jujitsu from Master Sokaku Takeda. Later he became a believer in Omotokyo which was a newly-risen Shinto religion of that time. He often told us that he arrived at realization during the practice of Omotokyo. At this time he founded Aiki-Budo. After World War II, he changed the name to Aikido since the word "Bu" could mistakenly be considered as martial or invading.

Aikido literally means the way to unify with Ki. Ki means the absolute universe. So Aikido means to become one with the universe. Before becoming one with the universe, one must unify his mind and body which were given from the universe. If the mind and the body are separated, it is impossible to become one with the universe.

Master Ueshiba often used phrases such as "KI NO NAGARE" (the flow of Ki) and "KI MUSUBI" (the harmony of Ki) but he lectured only on the text of Omotokyo or used the names of gods. He never explained what Ki was or how to understand Ki. He only expressed the workings of Ki through his beautiful and powerful techniques.

After he passed away in 1969, his followers only practised the Aikido techniques forgetting the Ki principles or workings of Ki which cannot be seen. I always taught "Ki training" meaning a way to unify mind and body to become one with the Ki of the universe and from this basis taught techniques. However other instructors could not understand Ki. So I established Shin-Shin Toitsu Aikido (Aikido with mind and body unified) in 1975.

This time my successor, Koretoshi Maruyama, is going to publish a book of Aikido based on his long training and experience in teaching both in and outside of Japan.

Many countries have a problem of violence in schools and youth resistance but no one has shown a solution to the problem. The twenty-first century will be on the shoulders of those young pupils.

There are those who try to establish a single philosophy to control society. In this, there is a danger of fascism. However teaching the principles of the Universe causes no harm. The Four Basic Principles to Unify Mind and Body are the principles of the universe which everyone can understand. Naturally Shin-Shin Toitsu Aikido, which is based on the Four Basic Principles, is also a principle of the universe. Thus teaching Shin-Shin Toitsu Aikido is not the forcing of one philosophy on others but is a way by which each person can return to the universe. Mr. Maruyama has made the curriculum of Aikido so that the instructors can teach it to the pupils at school. Naturally unification of mind and body is a way that businessmen, artists, sportsmen, and every other person can apply in their daily life. It can also help the sick and unfortunate people. But this time he has specially emphasized the education of young pupils. I hope all teachers, parents, and students will read this book.

KOICHI TOHEI

PREFACE

PREFACE

My teacher, Koichi Tohei, reached the understanding that mind and body are one. After long and difficult training he established the Four Basic Principles for Unification of Mind and Body, in order to communicate this understanding to others. These principles, and their application to the art of Shin-Shin Toitsu Aikido, will be explained in this book. When performed with coordination of mind and body, Aikido is an art which enables one to lead others freely by using these same principles. Master Koichi Tohei has written many books on this subject. This book hopes to demonstrate that Aikido is an art based on mind and body unification. Without this foundation, it is impossible to really learn Aikido.

We have many problems today in education. Violence in the schools is increasing at an alarming rate. Aikido can contribute to the solution of this problem, and thereby improve the quality of education. Both teachers and pupils should carefully consider that before controlling others, one must first control oneself. One should be strong enough to live calmly in all circumstances. The author hopes that this book will lead both teachers and youth in the way of mind and body coordination. Only through this understanding can we put an end to the problem of violence in our schools.

KORETOSHI MARUYAMA

AIKIDO with KI

CONTENTS

Sixth Level

PART ONE
Unification of Mind and Body

Chapter 1 / The Immovable Mind

Education today has become very difficult. Every day we hear about violence on university campuses and the many problems of young people. The teachers blame the parents, while the parents accuse the teachers of not doing their job. Each assumes that it is the responsibility of the other, so in the end the problem remains unsolved.

The real problem lies in the attitude of the adults. However bad a person may be, he was innocent at birth. A recent television program featured a conversation between the announcer and some delinquent boys. The announcer asked the kids if they would have behaved violently had they really trusted their teachers. The boys replied that they would have behaved correctly if they had had good teachers. Their violence stems from a loss of faith in parents, teachers, and society. There are many influences in society which contribute to the problem. Television, films, and magazines expose young people from an early age to murder and other acts of violence. When I was a child, television did not exist. We had to go to the cinema to see films. We needed the permission of our parents to go to the cinema. Parents could choose what was good for their children. Today nearly every home has a television, which continually excites children with displays of sex, violence, and amoral behavior.

We cannot expect politicians to change society. Only if parents, teachers, and children understand the situation, will they know what to do and learn to act properly. We were all born from our mother's womb. Most people think that they were created only by the sexual union of their parents. But we must think deeper than that. Many people who want children are not able to have them. There are also many unwanted children whose conception was not planned. No child is born of its own will. The survival of the human race is ensured by the love between men and women. Even animals do not act against the preservation of their own species. Children are born by the will of the Universe. A mother keeps the baby in her womb for nine months. Both parents work hard to bring up the child after birth. It is only natural that we be grateful to our parents for all of this. On the other hand, many parents mistakenly believe that they possess their children. They try to mold their children according to their own desires. Children are left in their parents' charge for a period of time, but they are not the possessions of their parents. Parents have no right to force their children to do only what the parents want. If one is entrusted with something, it is important to take care of it. When parents are entrusted with a baby, they have a duty to raise the child with care. Parents should understand this fact, and should talk to the baby from the very first. Even though an infant can not understand the words, he will understand the parent's affection. Communication is not done only through words. Even dogs understand the affection of people. Naturally a baby can understand its parents. If parents would talk to their babies in a positive manner, their children would never grow into bad people. If parents would speak positively, saying "You are a good boy," it will penetrate into the child's subconscious mind. If the parents even think, "You are not good," this will also penetrate into the baby's mind, and he will grow up likewise.

Instant food has become very popular. Many parents serve instant food to their children at home. But even food is transformed by our attitude toward it. However tired the parents may be, if they attend to the quality and preparation of what their children eat, the children will benefit from both the food and the affection. I met a school teacher the other day who told me the following story. The mother of one of her pupils came to visit her. While they were talking the teacher mentioned that she always prepared breakfast at home for her husband, children, and mother before coming to school. The mother's reaction was, "Oh you are so old fashioned. I buy breakfast in the supermarket nearby because it is already open at 7 o'clock in the morning. I hardly ever cook at home." She was proud of her beautifully manicured fingernails. Hearing this, the teacher became very sad for the child's future.

Parents today usually do not put their own minds into the education of their children. They prefer the easy way. Naturally some children turn to their teachers for affection. But many teachers cannot be trusted either. So groups of depressed children come together and retaliate against the society which has rejected them. There are very few teachers who try to see things from the children's point of view, to try to help them solve their problems. Many teachers only devote their attention to intelligent or cooperative pupils, ignoring the ones they believe are bad or unintelligent.

Some of these so-called bad pupils from the secondary school were recently interviewed on a television program. When one boy was caught smoking in the corridor of the school, the teacher only glanced at him, and continued on, saying nothing. Then he returned with some other teachers and began scolding the boy. The boy was unhappy because instead of scolding him immediately, the teacher brought other teachers to gang up on him. The boy reacted violently because of the cowardly attitude of the teacher. If the teacher is afraid of being hit by the boy, he can not educate him. He should scold the boy even at the risk of being hit. The boy will not hit the teacher if he respects him. He reacted violently because the teacher was not courageous enough to earn his respect.

Most teachers do not have the energy to truly educate the children. There are teachers who complain, saying, "Teachers are also professionals. We are working for money. Our salaries should be increased." Such teachers will not be able to educate children. Naturally they need enough money to live. But rather they should say, "We are educating the children who must carry the country into the future. We should have a respectable salary."

In ancient Japan people praised others by saying, "He has a good stomach." To speak ill of others people said, "His stomach is black. He has a small stomach." In the modern age we praise by saying, "He is smart. He is intelligent." Or we criticize by saying, "He is foolish." But when we judge people by their intelligence, we ourselves become mentally small. The author hopes that readers will learn more than just Aikido techniques from this book. What is real calmness? How does one find the immovable mind? This book will explain how to attain true calmness and immovable mind through the art of Aikido.

Teachers bear the responsibility for educating children. Young people bear the responsibility for the future of the world. I hope teachers and students alike will read this book and practice its techniques. That which one learns with the body is not easily forgotten. Through Aikido one can learn to live with a positive attitude in any situation.

Chapter 2 / Four Basic Principles to Unify Mind and Body

From ancient times unification of mind and body has been said to be most difficult. People have gone into the mountains to practise zazen, some practiced meditation under waterfalls, as well as many other techniques. There have been many who taught about unification of mind and body. But those who taught about the mind forgot the body and those who taught about body forgot the mind. That is why unification of mind and body has been very difficult.

The mind has its principles and the body has its own separate principles. Through the understanding of both principles one can live keeping mind and body unified. Master Koichi Tohei established the Four Basic Principles to Unify Mind and Body.

1. Keep one point.
2. Relax completely.
3. Keep weight underside.
4. Extend Ki.

Number one and four are principles of the mind and number two and three, principles of the body. All four are different descriptions of the same state, unification of mind and body. That means if one principle is maintained, the other three are automatically satisfied. If one is lost, then the other three are also lost. First I will explain the fourth principle, extend Ki .

EXTEND KI

A puts his right foot forward and extends his right arm forward. A then puts strength in his right arm so that B cannot bend his arm. B holds A's right wrist from underneath with his right hand and puts his left hand on the upper part of A's elbow and tries to bend A's right arm toward A's shoulder. If B is strong enough, he can easily bend A's arm.

Next A relaxes his arm and imagines his right arm is a fire hose in which water is rushing out from the fingertips. As A is imagining his arm is a hose, his mental energy is rushing out from his fingertips. B will not be able to bend A's arm (photo 1, 2).

This is usually called the unbendable arm. When using the imagination to cause mental energy to flow outward, we call it extending Ki. Light has light waves and sound has its own waves. Naturally the mind must also have mental waves. We only do not see them with our eyes. As long as A thinks and believes his mental energy is rushing out from his fingertips infinitely, then it really is rushing out. We normally forget it only because we do not see it with our eyes. The mind moves the body. One single thought can create tremendous power. When one understand this, then one must change the basis of training. One must change negative thoughts into positive thoughts.

Next B stands to one side as A walks past B. If A is thinking backwards as he walks, B will be able to make A fall by putting his arm in front of A's neck as A walks by. Now A walks by B again but thinking forward as he walks. B tries to make A fall as before but as long as A is thinking forward B will be dragged by A (photo 3).

When one goes to a place where one loves to go, one does not get tired since the mind is going forward. On the other hand if one is going to a place where one does not want to go, one gets very tired. There is a great difference between unification of mind and body and separation of mind and body. If one does what one loves to do, one progresses greatly without getting tired. So if one has to do something, one must extend Ki to it. To extend Ki is to have a positive spirit.

3

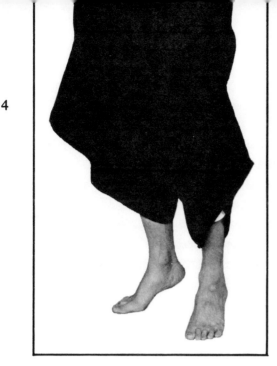

4

5

KEEP ONE POINT

Sometimes one misunderstands extending Ki. Putting strength in any part of the body to feel strong is a mistake. When one extends Ki, one's eyes and face are soft and calm and the body is relaxed.

A stands putting strength in any part of his body, for example, in the lower abdomen. Most people feel this is a strong posture. B pushes on A's left shoulder. A will easily lose his balance.

Next A stands naturally on his toes (photo 4). A can feel all his weight on his big toes and the weight of his upper body settles at a point about 10 cm below the naval. One should not put strength in the abdomen. The one point is lower than the place where one can put strength. There is a point where it is impossible to put strength even if one wants to. That is one point.

A keeps this state and calmly lowers his heels to the floor without moving his weight backwards. The weight of the upper body must always be at the one point. A should also imagine his one point is the center of the universe (photo 5). In this case A will be immovable even if B pushes. A from the front or the back. The immovable mind makes an immovable body. The one point in the lower abdomen is a place to put the immovable mind.

The one point is also thought of as being the center of the universe, which is infinite in all directions. So A imagines that he becomes the center of the universe. Even if A moves one step in any direction, because he is the center, the universe is still infinite in all directions. By understanding this, one will have a large heart and always be positive. This is real calmness.

A stands with left foot forward. B pushes A's left shoulder very hard (photo 6). If A puts strength in his body, he will lose his balance. Next A keeps one point and relaxes. When B pushes very hard, A's body will naturally turn to the left and B will lose his balance (photo 7). If the axle in figure 1 is fixed, and the ring turns the direction of the power, the axle will remain calm. If one keeps one point, the body moves very easily and even if an opponent attacks, one can move freely without disturbing his one point.

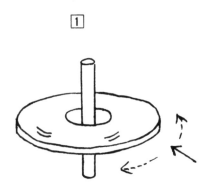

1

6

7

Keeping one point does not mean always being immovable. If one is pushed gently, naturally one is stable and calm. If B pushes A very hard, A can move keeping one point. This is an example of the principle of non dissension in Shin-Shin Toitsu Aikido. If A does not collide with B's power, it returns to B and B has to deal with it. Consequently B will lose his balance and fall. Succeeding without fighting is his best way. The best way of succeeding is to lead the opponent's mind without colliding. In Shin Shin Toitsu Aikido we always practise leading the opponents' mind.

8

A sits on his knees. B pushes A's chest with his right hand. If A does not keep his one point, A will easily fall backward.

9

A then raises his hips and relaxes his body by swinging his arms (photo 8). Next A sits down softly and again relaxes his body by swinging his arms (photo 9). B pushes A's chest with his right hand. This time A will not budge. B can also test A by trying to lift A's hands or knees. As long as A keeps his one point and relaxes, A will be immovable. In this state the weight of A's body is naturally underside (photo 10, 11).

10

11

So far I have explained how to relax in the standing or sitting position. This is the unification of mind and body. If one tenses either his mind or body, it is not unification of mind and body.

The earth is spinning around the sun. If there were no terrestrial gravitation, that is centripetal force, nothing could exist on earth. Everything on earth exists through the harmony of centrifugal force and centripetal force. That is why the natural posture is to keep one point with relaxation. If one tries to lower one's body, he breaks the harmony between the centrifugal and centripetal force. When one unifies one's mind and body, the weight of his body goes to its lowest part. Calmness is power. Calmness means the weight of every part of the body settles down to its lowest part. It does not mean to push one's body down.

Now let's practise how to keep one point while moving. A stands up from the sitting position. B pushes A's shoulder when A is in the weakest posture. If A loses his one point, he will fall down. B can also test A while A is kneeling down from the standing position (photo 12). If A stands up or sits down keeping one point, he will not lose his balance when pushed. Though one knows how to keep one point in the standing or sitting position, most people lose the one point during movement. When an elevator goes down, because the body also goes down, one feels that his mind goes up. The same thing happens when one sits down. The correct way is that the one point must go up or down and the body follows it. Every movement must be started from the one point. If one walks forward, the one point must move forward and the body follows it. Then the mind and the body are always unified. One must practise this in every day activities.

12

Now let's think more deeply to understand the one point. The one point in the lower abdomen is the center of the universe. But one is not the only center of the universe. Everything is the center of the universe. The universe is an infinite circle with an infinite radius. A finite circle has only one center but an infinite circle can have infinitely many centers.

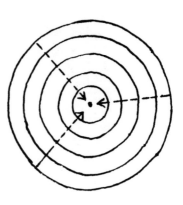

This infinite circle is condensed to become oneself and condensed further becomes the one point in the lower abdomen (fig. 2). This one point is not a tangible point but infinitely becomes smaller. Even when the one point is so small that one does not feel it any more, one should not stop its movement. One should leave it moving. Ki is the infinite gathering of infinitely small particles. This infinitely small movement is the calmness and the real meaning of the one point in the lower abdomen. When the one point is too small to feel , if one stops this movement of becoming smaller, it becomes dead calmness. Living calmness is the strongest state containing infinite movement and dead calmness is the weakest state without movement. The two look similar but are fundamentally different. Please see "Ki in Daily Life" written by Master Koichi Tohei for detailed explanations.

It is desirable to spend ten minutes daily sitting calmly while keeping one point. By sitting calmly ten minutes a day, one will be able to extend Ki in one's work and studying, etc. When one goes out, one must extend Ki forward so that one unifies one's mind and body. When one takes a meal, one must keep one point and eat. Then his Ki goes to the food and one tastes well and can digest very well. If one's mind is elsewhere, one does not taste well and the food taken will not be as nourishing. If the mind is elsewhere, one does not see, does not hear, and does not taste. If one puts one's mind to the meal, then all the food has its own taste and will be nourishing.

13

14

RELAX COMPLETELY

Many modern illnesses are caused by nervous problems. As civilization develops, one tends to be neurotic and irritated by complicated human relationships and hectic business practices resulting in ulcers of the stomach or heart attack. In that case the doctor will tell the patient to relax. But many doctors also get ulcers or have heart attacks. It is very difficult to relax all the time in this modern life. Most people think it impossible to relax all the time. However, if one can keep one point in the lower abdomen, it is easy to relax oneself.

A keeps one point and shakes his hands as quickly as possible (photo 13). It is important that the body shakes all over with the one point as the center so that all the tension is dispersed. If A puts strength in his hands, he cannot shake them quickly. That is why by shaking the body quickly, one can relax oneself. Some think that putting strength is slow but strong and that relaxation is quick but weak. This idea is wrong. One becomes weak not because one relaxes but because one stops one's Ki. The real relaxation is the strongest state.

A stands relaxed. B tries to push up A's wrist toward A's shoulder. A might be unstable even if he keeps balance. Next A keeps one point and shakes the whole body for 20 to 30 seconds. This time A will not budge even if B tries to push up A's wrist (photo 14). Shaking the hands very quickly means to relax completely. When one

15

relaxes completely, the mind is very calm at the one point in the lower abdomen. This is the strongest state.

A stands tensing his body. B tries to lift A's body at the underarms. If B is strong enough, he will be able to lift A. Next A shakes the body very quickly for 20 to 30 seconds. This time B will not be able to lift A (photo 15).

A shakes his hands and then swings up his arm. The arm is naturally unbendable. This means by relaxing completely, one naturally extends Ki without thinking about it.

A sales man had better do this relaxation exercises before visiting clients since one tends to be tense before important talks. A student or pupil might well do this relaxation exercises before examinations. Then they will be able to stay calm during the examinations.

KEEP WEIGHT UNDERSIDE

The weight of every object is at its lowest part. The human body is also an object so the weight of every part of the human body goes naturally to its lowest part. That is calmness. If one relaxes, one is calm. If one keeps one point, one can relax. If one relaxes, the weight of the whole body is underside. The four principles are different descriptions of the same thing.

16

A puts his right arm forward. B pushes up A's
upper arm. If A tenses his arm or thinks of the
upper side of the arm, B will be able to push up
A's arm. Next A relaxes his arm and thinks of the
lower side of this arm. B will not be able to lift it
easily (photo 16).

Shin-Shin Toitsu Aikido is not just the practice
of techniques. Technique alone will not make a
fine human being. By training oneself through the
principles of mind and body unification, one can
build a fine charactor and become one with the
universe. That is real strength.

PART TWO
Shin-Shin Toitsu Aikido
Techniques

The founder initiates the author into the deepest understandings of swords.
(1)

First Level

1. UDEMAWASHI UNDO

17

18

A stands naturally keeping one point. He then raises his left arm (photo 17) and lets it swing down imagining that the weight of his arm is on the underside (photo 18). If his arm is relaxed, the elbow will be naturally bent. The left arm goes up above the head as a reaction. When it is above the head, A's Ki must be extending up-ward (photo 19). A continues the swinging movement. He swings four times with the left arm and then the right arm for a total of two sets.

There is a rhythm in all the movements of the universe, the move-ment of the sun and the moon, the flow of water, the wind, etc. Without this rhythm all is powerless. Same is with the swinging of the arms. The weight of the arm is on its underside so when it comes down, the speed increases. When it goes up, it slows. However, most people put strength in the arm when they swing it up. In that case they have no power when the arm comes down. Then they try to force down the arm, which can injure the shoulder or the elbow.

When the arm comes down, the speed increases and with this rhythm the arm goes up again, then it comes down with energy. This rhythm works like a pendulum. One can perform every movement in sports very energetically with this rhythm.

When A's arm is down, B holds A's wrist and pulls it downward. If A keeps one point and relaxes his arm, he will be very stable. B pushes it upward toward A's shoulder. A will be stable in this case, too (photo 20). But if A forces down his arm, B will be able to move A very easily.

Next A swings both arms forward four times, then swings them backwards four times. He does this twice. Then he does the same thing but with lowering his hips when the arms come down. One can use this movement in all the techniques of Shin-Shin Toitsu Aikido. It is also relaxing and helps promote health. One must try this exercise often.

19

20

2. UDEFURI UNDO

A stands naturally keeping one point. He swings both arms to the left at the count of "One" (photo 21). The edge of the right hand and arm must be facing forward. At the count of "Two", he swings his arms to the right. A repeats these movements following the rhythm of the count. However vigorously he swings his arms, he must keep one point. If he keeps one point, his shoulders will not raise up (photo 22). B pushes A's shoulder in the direction A swings his arms. A will be very stable if he keeps one point (photo 23).

3. UDEFURI CHOYAKU UNDO

A swings his arm to the right and steps forward with his left foot (photo 24). Then at the count of "One", he swings his left arm forward (photo 25) as he steps forward with his right foot (photo 26). Continuing to swing both arms to the left, he pivots on the ball of his right foot. Then A steps back with his left foot and draws his right foot back. He should now be facing the opposite direction (photo 27). At the count of "Two", A reverses the motion of count "One". He swings his right arm forward as he steps forward with his left foot. Continuing to swing both arms to the right, he pivots on the ball of his left foot. He steps back with his right foot and draws his left foot back. He should now be facing in the original direction.

When A swings both arms to the left and stops with them in that position, his face and right shoulder should be facing in the same direction. If A is extending Ki to the direction of his face and right shoulder, he will be immovable even if B pushes his right shoulder (photo 28). A repeats these movements following the rhythm of the count. Keeping his arms relaxed and the center of his body stable are what enables A to swing his arms powerfully.

4. SAYU UNDO

Facing forward, A stands with his feet spread about shoulder width apart. He then swings both arms to the left at the count of "One". His face and torso should remain facing forward. The palms of both hands should be facing up. His left hand should be almost the same as or a little higher than the shoulder. The right hand stays in front of the torso (photo 29). With his upper body still facing forward, A lowers his hips by slightly bending his left leg. A's whole body will lower and move a little to the left on the count of "Two". His right leg should be extended naturally (photo 30).

In the postures shown in photo 30, A should not move if his right shoulder is pushed to the left. He will be immovable if he keeps one point and relaxes both arms completely, and keeps the upper part of his body straight. A's arms should not come up even if B tries to raise his arms from below. They will easily be pushed up if he tenses them, but if he relaxes and imagines the weight to be underside, his arms will be very heavy (photo 33).

When throwing B with "KATATETORI TENKAN KOKYUNAGE", A must move his arms as he did in SAYU UNDO described above.

Standing in the right hanmi (a posture in which one foot is forward), B leans his upper body back and keeps one point. He should be completely relaxed. Standing on B's right in left hanmi, A steps to the right behind B with his left foot and places his left arm

32

33

across B's chest. He tries to move B's body but B
will not fall as long as he keeps one point. Now A
applies the principles of SAYU UNDO. He relaxes
imagining the weight of his arm is underside. A
moves from his one point and lowers his whole
body to the left. This time A can move B quite
easily (photo 34, 35).

34

35

36

37

5. KOHO TENTO UNDO (1)

From the left hanmi, A sits down calmly with his one point. His legs are crossed and his hands rest naturally upon his thighs (photo 36). On the count of "One", A rolls backwards keeping his legs in the same position (photo 37). Then on the count of "Two" he should roll forward to his original position (photo 38). When A has returned to the upright sitting position, B stops him by pushing A's shoulders to the rear. If only A's body returns to its original position without his mind also being directed forward, A will fall backwards if B pushes on his shoulders. While rolling forward, if A directs his mind forward, he will not fall backwards when B pushes him (photo 39).

38

39

Since the mind moves the body, A's mind should be directed backwards as he rolls backwards and should be directed forward when he rolls forwards. This is a way of unifying the mind and the body. When reading a book, if A thinks about other things, he will not understand the content. he can only understand it if he directs his Ki to the book. In the same way when the face is forward, his Ki should also be directed forward. Most people use their minds and bodies separately. Their bodies are doing something while their minds are elsewhere. In this way they lose concentration. As industrialization develops and the economic life becomes rich, the human being is busy dealing with machines. In their daily lives people approach it only half-heartedly, for example eating while watching TV or studying while listening to music. In this way they use their minds and bodies separately so they lose their natural strength. Because of this many people have nervous breakdowns. One must always use his mind and body together.

40

41

KOHO TENTO UNDO (2)

Next A rolls backwards on the count of "One" and rolls forward and up to a standing position on the count of "Two". When A stands up straight, he will naturally be in left hanmi (photo 40, 41, 42). A practises this rolling exercise several times to the repeated count of "One" and "Two". At the moment A tries to stand, B with his left hand, pushes A's left shoulder down in an attempt to prevent A from standing up (photo 43).

If A thinks he is being held down by the shoulder when B is pushing on his shoulder, A will lose his one point. This is because A has stopped his Ki flowing at his shoulder by thinking the same. Consequently he will not be able to stand and will fall backwards instead. Instead of being worried about B trying to stop him, A should continue to extend his Ki strongly forward. And since the mind moves the body, this time A will be able to stand easily and B will lose his balance instead of A.

When one starts a business, one has a strong Ki even if one has some difficulties. However after the business is going well, one tends to slack his Ki. Then his business also goes down. Most important thing is to extend Ki.

Many students who do not do well at school think already, " I cannot do it," when they face a problem.

A keeps one point and says, "I can". Then he rolls backwards and stands up. B will not be able to prevent him.

Next A says "I cannot," and rolls. B will easily be able to stop A. Teachers must understand well this exercise so that they can give real confidence to students.

One must always use positive words and positive ideas in order to live a positive life.

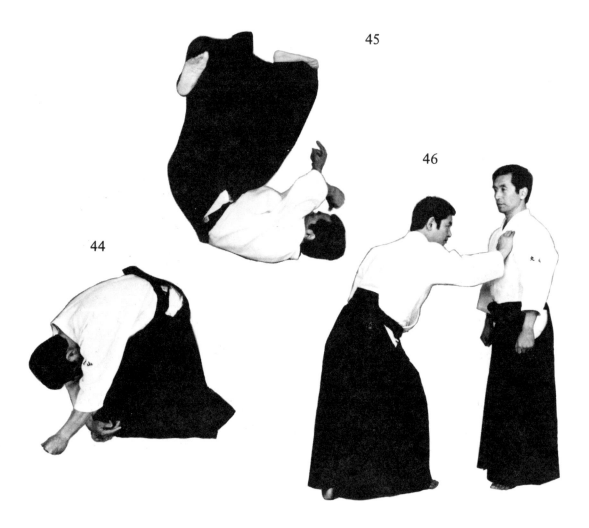

6. ZEMPO KAITEN UNDO

With his left foot forward, A bends forward and places his left hand, back of hand down, on the mat in front of his left foot. A puts his right hand down between his left hand and left leg (photo 44).

Tucking his head fully as if to cover it with his right arm and slowly moving his hips forward, A rolls over (photo 45). Continuing his roll, A sits up facing forward.

A continues rolling over and over like a rolling ball. In the beginning just two or three forward rolls will make A dizzy. But with a little practice he will be quite steady even after rolling around a large dojo. What he must do is calm his mind by keeping one point for a few seconds right after rolling, then he will be able to recover his balance. A should be stable even if pushed by B (photo 46).

7. KATATE KOSATORI KOKYUNAGE

Standing in right hanmi, A holds out his right hand. Also standing in right hanmi B grips A's right wrist with all his strength. If A tenses his right hand and tries to move it, he will find it difficult since his force will collide with B's force (photo 47).

Next A fully relaxes his right arm and also keeps one point. In such a state A can move his right hand easily and B will be unable to stop him from doing so. With this example A can understand that relaxation is the real strength. If someone is very angry at you, you can return his irritation back to him by keeping one point calmly. But if you also get angry, you receive his Ki. It is better not to receive bad Ki. However, not to receive Ki is different from putting up with something. If you put up with something, some day your anger will come out.

B grips A's right wrist tightly with all his strength. Taking a half-step behind B with his left foot, A grasps the back of B's neck with his left hand and then swings his right hand up in an effort to throw B backward. But if A tenses his arm, it will collide with the force of B's arm and he will be unable to throw B.

A keeps one point and fully relaxes his arm. Now he will find that B is unable to stand up against him. B will fall over when A swings his right hand over as if to stroke B's face downwards (photo 48).

In this way, even if A's wrist is held by B with all his strength, A can throw B if he relaxes completely. As long as B is tense and holds tightly with just physical strength, A does not need any particular technique to throw him. But what if B were to hold correctly, that is softly and with Ki extended?

Relaxing his arm and keeping one point, B holds A's right wrist lightly in his right hand. Though he holds lightly, B should be holding with Ki. B's Ki must flow through his fingers and envelop A's wrist. Then A will be unable to withdraw his hand from his grasp easily. Moreover since B keeps one point, A can neither push nor pull away from B. Unlike what happened in photo 48, A will not be able to throw B so easily. This time A must use the techniques of KOKYUNAGE and apply the principles of non-fighting to throw him (photo 49).

A extends his fingers and directs his Ki to flow through them strongly. Without moving his right wrist, he steps behind the right side of B by taking a step with his left foot. At the same time A grasps the back of B's neck with his left hand. In this position B's right arm and A's fingers should naturally be pointing in the same direction as if they were a couple pointing to and admiring the same scenery. At this time both A and B's Ki join and flow together (photo 50). In this position A's body must be touching B's body just a little. Thereby making this point of contact the center of a circle and his right arm its radius, A turns to the right and draws a circle with his fingers. Because their Ki flows together B will follow him without any resistance. However if A and B are separated and their bodies are not touching, there will be two centers. Consequently A will not be able to draw a circle. A can lead B easily only because they are united and their Ki flows together in the same direction, that is, because there is just one center (photo 51).

52

53

54

After making a circle to the right, A lowers his hips and points downward with his fingers. As long as A extends Ki strongly, B will follow his lead without resisting (photo 52).

Now A draws a circle in a diagonal plane. He continues the arc of his fingers so that they point upward (photo 53). Then finally A points to a spot between B's eyes. In this case A should not bend his wrist inside but rather stretch the side of the little finger so that the back of the hand faces A's own face. That is the whole arm makes a smooth curve. With his fingers pointed at B, A lowers his hand as if to thrust his fingers between B's eyes. But instead A's fingers skim past the left side of B's face and down towards the ground. As B's right hand falls with A's fingers B will also fall (photo 54).

The practice of Shin-Shin Toitsu Aikido may be compared to the practice of Japanese calligraphy. In calligraphy beginners start by writing simple lines and angles correctly. Then they write in the square style of Chinese characters. After mastering each character, they begin writing in the half cursive style and finally in the cursive style. Thus the calligraphers move through similarly graded states, perfecting each earlier step before attempting the next one. The letters are often written in the half-cursive or cursive style. But if this style is used only to save time and does not have the firm square hand as its foundation, the calligraphy will degenerate into a crabbed scrawl lacking any beauty. Similarly, the foundation is essential in the mastery of Shin-Shin Toitsu Aikido techniques. The beginning student learns how to hold or let others hold him, how to move his hips, hands, legs, and so on. After practicing these basic movements, he can combine them in various ways to learn the primary forms of the art. In principle and practice this stage is comparable to the square hand form in Japanese calligraphy. In the next step the student focuses on practicing movements with Ki, and thus enters the fluid form of Shin-Shin Toitsu Aikido. This style is equivalent to the half-cursive style in calligraphy. After the student has mastered this form, then he does not have to wait for the opponent to grab him. Instead when his opponent's Ki moves, he leads it and throws him. This final stage is the equivalent of the cursive style in Japanese calligraphy.

Actual occasions of writing or self-defense call for the half-cursive or more often the cursive style. Yet it is the firm, square hand which must be mastered carefully before using the other two styles. Otherwise the art, whether it be calligraphy or Shin-Shin Toitsu Aikido, will lack grace and power.

55

56

B stands in right hanmi and grasps A's right wrist. A tests B by pushing or pulling his right hand. If B keeps one point, his body is immovable.

Starting by letting his left arm swing behind himself (photo 55), A then swings his arm strongly forward as if to catch B by the back of his neck with it. In doing this A keeps one point so his hips and his right hand will naturally move to the right. A should extend strong Ki to the back of B's neck with his left hand so that B has the feeling that his neck is being pushed. Then instinctively he will follow the movement of A's right hand and sway his upper body forward (photo 56).

A thus understand how to move B by swinging both arms. Now A again starts in right hanmi and lets B hold his right wrist. The moment A swings his left hand behind B's neck, he leaps behind him. As his feet touch the ground, his left hand catches B's neck and A swings both arms down to lead B downward. A should not push down B's neck but swing both arms down in a relaxed way so that B's Ki moves downward. A then swings up his arms so that B will face upward and fall.

57

58

B faces A a few steps away. A stands in right hanmi and extends his right hand forward as if he were offering it to B. B grabs at it as quickly as he can. A quickly pulls his right hand in when B comes to grab it. But if B is fast enough he can still catch it (photo 57).

B comes to take A's extended hand once again. This time A extends his Ki strongly and swings his arm to the right. By doing this A will stop B from grabbing his hand, and at the same time start to lead him around to his right (photo 58).

59

A continues to lead B's hand. Finally A swings his right hand down (photo 59), and then up (photo 60). A points his right fingers toward B's face so that B falls backwards (photo 61).

Suppose water flows forth from an underground spring at the bottom of a lake. However small the spring may be, while it flows forth, no drop of water from the lake can force itself into the opening of the spring. But the moment its flow of water stops, the lake water will pour immediately into the opening. It is the same with Ki. While our Ki pours forth that of our opponent cannot enter and affect us. But once we pull or stop our Ki, our opponent's Ki will immediately come pouring forth at us. As long as we extend Ki, we need not worry even when attacked suddenly in the dark. The difficulty lies in extending Ki all the time. Therefore in Shin-Shin Toitsu Aikido we must constantly train ourselves to keep our mind calm, to keep one point, and extend Ki from every part of our body. In photo 57 A's pulling of his hand in was the physical form of his pulling Ki. Because in pulling his Ki, A received B's Ki, it was possible for B to take A's hand. In photo 58, instead of pulling in his right hand, A continued to extend and swing his hand to the right. Thus B's Ki could not enter since the circle drawn by A's hand is endless, B can never catch up with A's hand.

In our daily life we should always keep one point and extend Ki, so that we can live a happy strong life. Once we stop or pull our Ki, we are affected from outside and lead an unstable negative life.

60

61

62

63

64

8. KATATETORI TENKAN KOKYUNAGE

Standing in left hanmi, A holds out his left hand with his wrist fully bent. B stands in right hanmi and holds A's left wrist with his right hand (photo 62).

Keeping B's Ki directed where A's left fingers are pointing, A moves his hips closer to B. In doing so he should not push against B's strength with his left hand. A should only bring his hips closer to B, moving neither his left foot or wrist (photo 63).

Turning his hips to the right by pivoting on his left foot, A takes a step to the right behind B with his right foot (photo 64). Leaving his left arm as it is, A draws his left foot back to his right foot (photo 65). Notice, if A pulls in his left hand when he draws back his left foot, he pulls Ki and loses everything. Because A leaves his arm where it is when he draws his left foot back, his arm will be stretched naturally and fully. From this position A turns to the right in a circular movement, and causes B to follow him in the same clockwise direction (photo 66).

s hips at an appropriate
to lose his balance and
oto 67).
up his arms leading B's

ward B's face and bring
point. B will fall down

FIVE PRINCIPLES OF SHIN-SHIN TOITSU AIKIDO

We can understand the Five Principles of Shin-Shin Toitsu Aikido through these examples.

1. EXTEND KI

When A stands in left hanmi and holds out his left hand with his wrist fully bent, B tries to push A's left wrist toward his shoulder. If A is not extending Ki, he will be easily moved by B. When you start something, you must always extend Ki first. It is too late if you start and then extend Ki. You must first extend Ki and then start. If A is extending Ki, A will not be pushed by B.

2. KNOW YOUR OPPONENT'S MIND

A must know how B's Ki is moving. Without knowing your opponent's mind, it is difficult to succeed.

3. RESPECT YOUR OPPONENT'S KI

In this case we know B's Ki is coming toward A. Then A must respect this Ki. If A tries to move B's hand, B can resist very easily. So A must respect B's Ki by not moving B's hand and instead A moves his body next to B's.

4. PUT YOURSELF IN THE PLACE OF YOUR OPPONENT

There are people who say, "No, I don't agree." Even if you think someone is wrong, first try to understand his opinion. Every body has his own ideas and situations. You must put yourself in his place. One who is on top of a mountain and the other who is only half way see very different scenes. It is nonsense to disagree with each other. So A must put his mind and body in the same place as B's.

5. PERFORM WITH CONFIDENCE

If A puts himself in B's place, B will not have a fighting mind. Then when A turns his body in a circle, B will gladly follow. As A lowers his hips, B will also lower his hips. When A stands straight up, B again will follow. As A brings his hand and arm toward B's face, B will fall backwards. B will not feel like he was forced to fall but gently led into his fall.

Nowadays we have the problem of violence in schools. It is no use to try and oppress the students. The real problem is that the teachers have forgotten their responsibilities of teaching. They only think of protecting themselves from the violence of the students, which causes a fighting mind towards the students.

There was a school teacher in Hawaii who wanted to learn Aikido for self-defence because of the violence in school. Master Tohei taught him how to deal with the students using positive Ki. He then taught the school teacher Shin-Shin Toitsu Aikido with Ki principles. The students ceased to be violent and became very friendly toward the teacher. I visited him at his school and found the students respect and like him very much.

The Five Principles of Shin-Shin Toitsu Aikido are indispensable in leading others and must be practised through Aikido techniques. Teachers especially should not forget this.

70   71   72

Second Level

9. IKKYO UNDO

A stands in left hanmi. Lightly closing both fists, he allows them to hang naturally on both sides of his hips (photo 71).

Moving his hips forward at the count of "One," A swings his arm up along his sides and out to the front. While he does this, he opens the fingers of his hands (photo 70).

Swinging his hands down to his sides again, A moves his hips back at the count of "Two." As his arms swing down, he lightly recloses his hands (photo 71).

A practices this exercise repeatedly on the counts of "One" and "Two." He must practice this exercise standing in both the left and right hanmi position.

As A moves his hips forward and swings his arms up, B pushes forward on A's back with his right hand. If A tenses his arms, he will stagger forward at B's push.

If A staggers on being pushed from behind, he will stagger backwards if B stops his hands when they come to the top of their swing and pushes on them from the front with his hands.

A keeps one point and keeps both arms relaxed completely while swinging them up. Now he will be immovable whether B pushes him from the front or from behind (photo 72). But it is difficult for beginners to keep their arms and hands fully relaxed while raising them.

Standing in left hanmi, A swings his left hand forward and up. In doing this most people make the mistake of lifting their arm and hand from the shoulder, and thus tense that area unnecessarily. The correct way to swing the hand up is to move from the fingertips.

Imagine that A's left arm is a firehose. His Ki corresponds to the water running through the hose. If water is rushing out the hose, to change the direction of this water one would of course hold the nozzle of the hose and not the middle of the hose. If one held the middle, it would be too heavy and unwieldly to change the direction of the water. Similarly when A swings his arms up he must move from his fingertips.

When water flows freely and strongly out of the hose, the nozzle gives the most sensation to the touch. If the middle of the hose gives the most sensation, it indicates that the water has stopped flowing freely at that spot. When A swings his hands up, he should feel the most sensation in his fingertips and in the outer or little finger side of his hands. If A feels more sensation in the area of his shoulder and upper arm, it shows that his Ki has stopped at those places. At the command, "Extend Ki," many people often stretch their arms, raise their shoulders, and tense their shoulders, and tense their fingertips. But this is a mistaken reaction. Do not forget that Ki extends most powerfully in the state of complete relaxation.

Now A can practise this exercise in the following manner.

A stands in left hanmi, lightly closing both fists. At the count of "One" he extends Ki forward and up without moving his body.

At the count of "Two" he swings up his hands as he moves his hips forward. If he relaxes his arms completely they will naturally stop at eye-level.

At the count of "Three" he extends Ki downwards without moving his body. At the count of "Four" he brings down his arms to the hips as he moves his hips backwards.

The mind moves the body. However many people move their bodies first and their Ki follows. In this way A makes sure that he extends Ki first and his body follows.

73

74

10. ZENGO UNDO

On the count of "One" and "Two," A performs the same movements as in IKKYO UNDO (photo 73).

After A has lowered both hands and pulled back his hips on the count of "Two," he pivots 180 degrees to his right so that he now faces the opposite direction (photo 74, 75). As he pivots A keeps both fists close to his hips and does not move his legs. Moreover he must turn on the balls of his feet rather than the heels. If he turns on the heels, he will lose one point. A should now be standing in right hanmi.

On the count of "Three," A moves his hips forward and swings his hand up as in count "One," (photo 76).

On the count of "Four," A brings down both arms and pulls his hips back as count "Two" (photo 77).

Keeping both fists at his hips, A pivots 180 degrees to his left on the balls of his feet, and waits for the count to return to "One." He should now be in the same left hanmi posture he was in at the beginning.

On the count of "One" and "Three," A moves his hips forward. At this time B tests A by pushing either his hips or shoulders from behind. Most people are stable when tested on the count of "One" since they have already practiced remaining immovable in this

position in IKKYO UNDO. Yet these same people will stagger forward when pushed on the count of "Three." If they remain stable when tested on the count of "One," why do they readily lose their balance when tested on count "Three?"

They remain immovable when tested at the count of "One" because they have practiced how to extend Ki forward strongly in IKKYO UNDO. Naturally if their Ki extends fully, their one point remains undisturbed, and thus they are immovable. But why is this not the case on the count of "Three?"

At the count of "Three" all the Ki that was extended forward at the count of "One" must be redirected so as to flow fully and strongly in the opposite direction. If A faces another direction, his Ki should also be naturally extended in that direction. This is what it means to unify mind and body. Yet at the count of "Three," most people fail to change the direction of their Ki, and half or all of their Ki remains focused in the direction of count "One." Thus their Ki is not fully and strongly extended in the direction they are facing at count "Three." Extending Ki and keeping one point are one and the same. If one does not extend Ki in the direction he faces, he loses one point. Thus without his mind and body unified, A will stagger forward when B pushes him on the count of "Three."

A should practice directing all of his Ki forward when he faces forward, and all of it in the opposite direction when he turns around. In short in training the body to move, A must also train his mind to be capable of focusing in any direction instantly.

There is a saying which says, "Play well, learn well." This saying suggests that one should play hard when playing, and study diligently when studying. Playing well and learning well complement each other. If a child plays well, he will also study well. But to worry about studying when playing, means also to think about playing when studying. Doing things in this manner will only dissipate one's energies and make it impossible to accomplish anything.

Instead one should do things with mind and body unified. Doing things in this way means to immerse oneself into whatever one does. But this state of concentration and full commitment must not be mistaken with the state where the spirit is fixed and obsessed with one thing, thought or activity to the exclusion of others. This latter state only appears as a state of unification. In it the spirit is attached to what it is doing and is not free. Real unification entails freedom and fluidity, that is, the ability to turn the spirit completely to whatever activity becomes appropriate as situations change. It is the ability to play completely when the time is right for playing and to study completely when the time calls for learning. In the Aikido exercises real unification entails the ability to turn the mind immediately in the direction the body faces.

After playing outside, some children sit at their desks with their minds still wandering outdoors. At such times, these children cannot learn anything because their spirits are not directed to their studies. Naturally they will lose interest, become frustrated, and be tempted to give up studying. Let these children practice the ZENGO UNDO carefully to develop skill in changing the direction of the mind. The body will neither be strong or able to move quickly unless it is trained; so too, with the mind.

11. HAPPO UNDO

After having learned how to move to the front and back with mind and body unified, practice the following exercise to learn how to turn freely in any direction without losing the unification of mind and body. This exercise is called HAPPO UNDO.

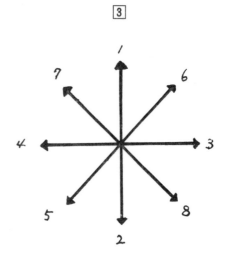

A stands in left hanmi with his fists hanging naturally at his side.

On the count of "One" A steps forward with his left foot while simultaneously opening his fingers and swinging his hands up as in IKKYO UNDO. A also draws his right foot up to his left

Then immediately lowering both hands and closing them lightly as they come down, A pivots 180° to his right on the balls of his feet. As he pivots he must keep his fists at his sides. Now A should be facing the opposite direction in a right hanmi position and be waiting for the count of "Two."

Taking a step forward on his right foot on the count of "Two," A swings both arms up from his sides as in count "One" and draws his left foot up to his right foot.

Then immediately lowering both hands to his sides, A turns 90° to his left and waits for the count of "Three." At the count of "Three," he steps forward with his left foot and draws his right foot up while simultaneously doing IKKYO UNDO with his arms. Lowering his arms he pivots 180° to his right so he now faces the opposite direction. on the count of "Four" he repeats the same sequence of movements as in the count of "Two." Now A has moved in four of the eight directions of this exercise. On the count of "Five" he steps 45° to his left and repeats the same sequence of movements as in the count of "One." To complete the eight directions on the count of "Six" he turns 180° to his right; on "Seven" he turns 90° to his left; on "Eight" he turns 180° to his right. After he turns A performs IKKYO UNDO in each direction. See the following diagrams for further clarification of the eight directions. The footwork consists merely of stepping left, right, left, right.

In ZENGO UNDO it is relatively easy to direct the mind forward or backward. Even doing IKKYO UNDO in eight directions as in this exercise is manageable when moving slowly, but to direct the mind and body in eight directions is very difficult when moving quickly. To see if the mind and body are unified and directed in the proper direction, try the following exercise.

1. In the beginning practice HAPPO UNDO slowly. Count slowly so that everyone will be able to follow.

2. Next pick a point at about eye level in each of the eight directions. Any point or mark will suffice, and one in each direction should be easily found whether the exercise be done outdoors or indoors. As you do HAPPO UNDO, try to see the point you've picked in each of the eight directions. The fact that the eye catches the mark is proof that your Ki has reached the mark. Since the eye will not be able to see the mark if your Ki is not directed in the same direction, testing yourself in this way will show you whether or not your mind and body were unified throughout the exercise. If you cannot see all of the eight points, you failed to maintain the unification of mind and body.

3. In the beginning make the count slow, and gradually make it faster. When the count is slow everyone should be able to see each point, but when the count is fast many become frantic in their movements and lose the coordination of mind and body. Then the eye will no longer be able to see the points.

4. Now instead of concentrating on moving the body, try to see the fixed mark the moment the count corresponding to it is given. Then the body will naturally follow the movement of the mind, and mind and body will move together. Even if the count is given quickly your Ki will reach the mark, and you will be able to follow the count easily. Worrying about the physical steps will not lead to success. Since the mind moves the body, once the mind has turned in the proper direction the body will follow.

Suppose A's full abilities and strength can be measured and that it is expressed by the number 10. Thus A can be said to have the power of 10 when he unifies his mind and body and fully commits himself to a task. In HAPPO UNDO if he turns his full power of 10 in the right direction at the count of "One," it means that he does his best. But on the count of "Two" if he leaves half of himself in the direction of "One," it means he faces the second direction with only the power of 5. His power will decrease further at the count of "Three." By the count of "Four" he will probably have lost all his power. This means that A is not using his full power of 10 as he goes through the exercise. It also means that A is not doing his best. A does his best only when he directs himself completely in each of the eight directions. With each count A must change the direction of his mind immediately, so that he faces each direction with his full power of 10. If he does this, it means that when he is attacked by several opponents, he will be able to deal with them freely. Even after throwing the first man who attacks, he will still have his full power of 10 available to handle a second or third opponent. Always able to do his best, A can be confident about dealing with any number of opponents.

It is the same in daily life. Anyone can deal with one difficult problem, but if three or four problems arise, he is at a loss. At these times he must use his ability to direct his mind freely and confront each problem as it comes. Since he will face each problem with his full power of 10, he should be able to solve each one in turn. But to be able to do this, continual training in moving and directing the mind is necessary.

12. ZENSHIN KOSHIN UNDO

A stands in left hanmi. He looks forward and extends Ki. He points forward with his right index finger at his right temple (photo 78). At the count of "One", he steps back on his left toes as far as possible (photo 79) and then moves his weight to his left foot and draws his right foot to the left. The index finger remains in the original position, which means his right arm must be extended (photo 80).

B pushes back A's hand. If A's Ki is extending forward, it will be immovable (photo 81).

Most people withdraw Ki when retreating. It is very important to extend Ki forward when the body is retreating.

Next at the count of "Two", he takes a small step on his right foot and a large step on his left, drawing his right foot to his left. He puts his index finger to the right temple, becoming the original posture. A tries the other side with the count of "Three," and "Four."

After repeating this exercise many times, A will understand how to retreat extending Ki forward. Then A practises the same movement without the index finger. B can now test A by pushing his shoulder.

When one is in good condition, one naturally extends Ki. It is important to extend Ki when one is in bad condition.

78　　　　　　　79　　　　　　　80

81

63

82

83

13. KOKYU DOSA

A sits on his knees keeping one point. He raises his hands with his fingers spread.

Also on his knees, B grabs A's wrists from their outer sides in his hands (photo 82).

Maintaining a strong extending of Ki through his hands, A moves his body straight forward. B will lose his posture and begin to fall backwards (photo 83).

If A thrusts his left hand out more than his right, B will lose his balance and fall to A's left. A follows B with his whole body as he falls (photo 84). Then A gently presses B's right wrist with his left hand and places his right hand lightly on the right side of B's chest.

64

85

Settling his mind at the one point, he keeps the weight of his hands and arms underside. Doing this makes A like an immovable rock, and B will be unable to throw A back or get up (photo 85).

In short A controls B with the power of mind and body unified, that is, with the power of his Ki. If A tries to hold B down only with physical strength, B will be able to throw him off easily. The correct way of holding an opponent down is described in Japanese as, "Ki de osaeru," that is, to hold down with Ki.

This exercise is not to be mistaken to be a physical pushing game. If it were, pushing against a pine tree in the garden would be more helpful for the muscles. The purpose of this exercise is to train Ki by extending it out strongly from the one point. To overthrow an opponent does not mean to use force on him, but to lead and eventually subdue his Ki with one's own strong Ki. To be able to do this we must first be able to control our own Ki. Therefore it is important to make A aware of his own state of mind and body.

A sits on his knees. If A is keeping one point, he will not move whether B pushes his shoulders from the front or from behind.

Next B tries to lift A's wrist. His wrist will not come up easily because his weight should be underside. Now B tries raising A's left knee with both hands. Again because weight is underside, his knee should not come up.

A raises his arms straight forward with the fingers spread apart. Just then B pushes back on A's chest. Even those people who were not moved by B's push when their hands were down, usually fall back on being pushed when they are raising them. It means that their way of raising them is incorrect.

Suppose water is shot powerfully out of a fire hose by a fire pump. In trying to change the direction of the water, we naturally hold the nozzle. So in raising his arms, if A relaxes them completely and moves them from his fingertips, his Ki will pour out powerfully from his fingertips. Moreover, if A does this, the weight of his arms will remain underside, and he will not move when B pushes his chest. But if A carelessly raises his hands from his shoulders or upper arms, he will lose one point (photo 86).

86

The one point is the pump; both his arms are the hoses, and the fingertips are the nozzles through which A's Ki is pouring forth. But in the position of photo 82, where B sits facing him and holds his hands, A's Ki cannot reach him yet. When the water from an actual fire hose cannot reach a real fire, there is no point in pulling the hose off from the pump in an effort to get it closer to the fire. The obvious thing to do would be to bring the fire pump itself nearer to the site of the fire. Similarly if A, sitting as he is, tries to push B down with only his hands, his efforts can be likened to carrying the hose close and leaving behind the pump. In this case A's Ki will be cut off.

A should stop moving his hands. Instead, he should move towards B from his one point. Then B will be effected by A's extending of Ki and fall down easily. If A forces B straight backwards as B falls his feet will come out toward A. But if A throws B as in photo 48, B's feet will go out to the side, and A need not worry about being kicked. Moreover it is easier for B to fall if A throws him this way. In throwing B down to the left, A may be tempted to use strength to push B with his right hand and to pull his right hand towards himself with his left hand. But A must not do this. If A extends Ki through his right hand but pulls Ki with his left hand, his right hand is like a plus force; and his left hand like a negative force. Consequently the net effect will be zero.

Sitting on his knees, A thrusts forward his left hand and lets B hold it. If A tries to push B's hand back, he will collide against B's force, and this exercise will become a contest of strength.

A does not let his left hand collide against B's right hand. Instead A moves his whole body forward while extending Ki straight through his left fingertips. His fingertips are directed slightly to the outside of B's body. Then B's body will sway backwards. At that moment if A cuts down with his left hand behind B on his right side, B will fall to that side.

This is to say that A's pushing B with his right hand or pulling him with his left hand does not make B fall. What makes him fall is A leading B's Ki toward his right and to the back. Then if A's right hand follows B, and if A extends it when B sways, B will fall all the more quickly.

14. KATATORI IKKYO

Standing in left hanmi, A exposes his left shoulder to B. Because it seems that he can easily grab it with his right hand, B attempts to do so (photo 87). At the moment when B's right hand is about to grab A's left shoulder, A steps back with his left foot and at the same time lightly redirects B's hand down with his own right hand. Then by drawing his right foot back to his left foot, A creates a space between B and himself (photo 88). A grasps B's right fingers in his right hand and swings B's right hand above his head (photo 89). Then swinging it down, A holds B's right upper arm down with his left hand (photo 90). If A then takes a step forward on his left foot and follows it forward with his right foot, he will lead B down to the ground with his face forward (photo 91).

If however, after A swings his right arm in a circle and holds it down, B calms himself at his one point and relaxes his right arm completely, then when A tries pushing B down, all of his force will be received at B's one point and flow out through his right leg. No matter how hard he tries, he will not be able to bring him to ground.

87

88

89

90

91

When this happens, A stops trying to forcefully push B down. He keeps the position of his hands the same, still holding B's right arm down. Then keeping his body erect, A directs his Ki straight forward and takes a big step forward on his left foot and immediately follows with his right. This will cause B to naturally fall forward. In this case A did not force B down, but instead led his mind. When practicing A must always concentrate on leading B's mind. Since A directed his Ki forward, B's mind is also led forward. Consequently when A's body goes forward, B's body follows without resistance. Since A is standing he can take a large step forward. On the other hand since B's body is bent forward, he cannot move his legs very well. If he wants to go forward, he must fall forward. In short, by first directing B's mind, A can bring him down to the ground without using any force at all.

The mind moves the body. While it may be hard to move an opponent's body, if you lead the mind, the body follows willingly. In the business world, if the boss only tells his men to work hard while not working himself, his men will grumble. If the boss works hard first then his men will follow him naturally.

EXERCISE

A can practise this same movement by himself. Standing in left hanmi, A brushes down his own left shoulder with his right hand on the count of one. At the same time he steps backward with his left foot then draws his right foot near, resulting in the right hanmi. The right hand is kept down with the small finger to the outside.

B tests A's right hand by lifting toward A's shoulder. If A's arm is tense, A will move easily. If A keeps one point and relaxes, his hand will be unliftable. A will repeat this part several times on each side. Next on the count of "Two" A swings both arms in a big circle. When both of A's arms swing down, A's hip is turned to the right so that the right hand is at the side of the right thigh and left hand is in front of the body. On the count of "Three" A takes a big step with his left foot forward. Then A kneels on his right knee and puts both hands on the ground. A must keep his toes bent. B tests A's shoulders by pushing backwards. If A is tense, A will fall backwards B can also push up A's hands. If A keeps one point and relaxes his arms, A will not move.

Try this whole exercise to the count of "One," "Two," and "Three" on each side.

The founder initiates the author into the deepest understandings of swords.

(2)

92

TENKAN

When B tries to grab his left shoulder, A withdraws his left foot and redirects B's right hand down with his right hand as he did in IRIMI (photo 92, 93).

Grapsing B's fingers, A swings B's right hand up above his face (photo 94).

A leaps behind B's right side (photo 95). Continuing this backward motion, A turns his hips strongly around to the right. At the same time A swings his right hand around and down to the right and follows this movement with his left hand (photo 96). B will be forced to spin around and down to the outside by these movements (photo 97).

A can do either KATATORI IKKYO IRIMI or TENKAN from the position in photo 88 and 93. If another opponent tries to hit him from behind, A can perform the TENKAN movement instead. Then the opponent will hit B's head rather than A's. Practise repeatedly IRIMI and TENKAN from the left side and right side.

EXERCISE

A can do the TENKAN exercise by himself. Standing in left hanmi, A counts one while brushing down his own left shoulder as he steps backwards.

93

94

At the count of "Two" he swings both arms up and steps forward with his right foot a little, and then follows with his left foot. As he turns he swings both arms down until both hands and the left knee touch the ground. A must be immovable even if B pushes up on A's hands or down on A's hips.

95

97

96

15. MUNETSUKI KOTEGAESHI

Standing in left hanmi, A turns the upper part of his body towards B so it seems that B can strike his chest easily. A waits for B to strike him (photo 98).

Taking a step forward on his right foot, B advances to strike at A's chest. At the moment before B's fist touches his chest, if A pivots on the ball of his feet and turns his hips to the right, B's fist will miss him and strike thin air (photo 99).

A turns his hips further to the right while stepping back to the right with his right foot. Simultaneously, he catches B's right hand with his left hand and leads it farther forward in the same direction that it is already travelling. B will be led off balance and will be caused to stagger forward and around A to the right by centrifugal force (photo 100).

A's left hand should hold and bend B's right wrist just as he passes in front of him. With his right hand on the back of B's right hand, he should follow the downward movement as B falls on his back (photo 101).

When B's body hits the ground, A immediately lifts B's right wrist with his left hand. At the same time A swings his right hand down and grasps B's right elbow with it (photo 102).

While keeping his hold on B's elbow and wrist, A walks around to the left. If B's right hand is kept over his head, the turning of the elbow will cause B to turn over on his face. To complete the throw, A holds B's right wrist inside his left elbow and with his hand,

98   99

100

101

slightly bends B's right elbow in the direction it normally bends. Then while thinking that B's arm is stuck to his body, A slowly turns his entire body toward B's head. When B feels a sharp pain in the shoulder area he must signal this by slapping the ground with his other hand. Then A must stop and release B from the hold (photo 103).

102

103

HIP MOVEMENT

Standing in left hanmi, A turns his body to B. B tries to strike A in the chest. A's feet are on the line of B's attack as illustrated in figure a. The arrow showing the direction of B's attack will naturally strike A (photo 104). However if A stands on his toes and twists his hips to the right, his feet will move off the line of B's attack as in figure b. Consequently his body is safe from attack. If A twists his hips a little, B's right hand will miss him completely (photo 105).

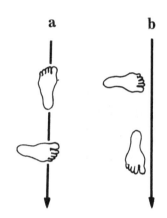

104

105

MA-AI

MA-AI is most essential when fighting for one's life; so much so that MA-AI can be the reason for vicotry or defeat.Briefly defined,MA-AI refers to the correct interval in terms of both distance and time between two parties. If one assumes the correct MA-AI, then neither the other person's fists nor his forward foot can reach him unless the other takes a step forward. In MA-AI one can be reached by the rear foot of the other, but to kick with that foot, the other would have to first shift his entire weight to his forward foot, which is the same as stepping forward.

If A stands where B can strike him with his right hand without having to move his feet, B can also reach him with his left hand or with his forward foot. Therefore B can strike with his right hand and quickly follow with a strike from his left hand. Or pretending to strike with his hand, B can then kick with his leg. Even if A initially succeeds in warding off each of these attacks with his hands or by twisting his body to the left or right, he will be unable to keep up such a flurry of activity for long. If A takes the correct MA-AI from the beginning, he need not do anything until B has advanced forward from his position. There is no need for A to worry about defending himself against that which cannot reach him, whether it be a punch or a kick.

A should calm himself by keeping one point, then he should check and hold back B's Ki by extending his own Ki steadily and powerfully. If he does this, he will be able to detect the faintest stirrings of B's Ki. Because the movement of B's Ki is clear as soon as B decides to step forward or to kick with his rear foot, A will have ample time to adjust himself and prepare for his next move.

If B advances towards A, little by little decreasing the distance between them, A can maintain the proper MA-AI by retreating little by little. A must be certain ,however, to continue to extend Ki as he does this. If B retreats, A can follow after him to preserve the MA-AI. If B tries to destroy the MA-AI suddenly, A can leap in and throw him or pin him on the spot. In Aikido, one should practice in this manner so that from the MA-AI position, it is always possible to leap right behind the opponent.

The following examples will explain how to detect the movement of B's Ki even before he actually moves his body.

After creating MA-AI between himself and B, A stands in left hanmi. From his left hanmi position, B suddenly steps forward on his right foot and strikes at A's chest with his right fist. Since this is only practice, he does not actually hit him but stops his fist just before contact. Since A will have no fear of being struck by B in this exercise, he must practice remaining immovable and calm. A should concentrate on remaining both physically and spiritually still. He should not move so much as an eyebrow. A can easily do this if he maintains one point. If he does not, he will flinch and carelessly pull his Ki when B strikes with a sudden attack. A must cultivate a perfectly calm spirit by remaining absolutely still while he lets B strike at him as quickly as he can.

When the mind is perfectly still, it is like the flat surface of absolutely calm water or like a well polished mirror. However quick a movement may be, it cannot pass in front of a mirror without being reflected in it. So, however quick an opponent's movement may be, they cannot escape the eye of the spirit if the mind is perfectly calm.

After having practiced keeping calm in this manner A then sharply says, "Yes!" the moment he perceives that B is going to strike. If B's hand is already at A's chest when he says, "Yes!" it means that A would have been struck by B had this been an actual fight. This means that A has been watching for the movement of B's hand instead of concentrating on perceiving the movements of B's Ki, and consequently is slow to respond and is hit by B.

Since the mind moves the body, B must first be motivated to strike. This desire to strike, initiates the movement. However quickly B may try to strike A, there will be time between the moment his Ki arouses him to attack and the moment his right hand reaches A's chest. If A practices in this manner, he will then see that B's hand reaches him a little later than the moment he says, "Yes!" With this split second advance warning, it will be easy for A to ward off B's hand or to turn his body away. A must practice this exercise until he has learned this timing well.

This time B takes a step forward and makes an actual attempt to strike A's chest. Instead of saying, "Yes!" and without moving his body, A strikes the top of B's wrist down with his left arm the moment before it reaches his body. If A strikes swinging his left arm first up, then down, he will be too late, and B will strike his chest. There is no need for an upward "one" movement to generate power for the downward "two" movement if A keeps one point and if his entire body is relaxed. In this state the weight of his left arm will naturally be underside, making it extremely effective when he strike down with it. If A tries to strike powerfully, he will tense his arm and his movements will be inhibited. Consequently striking B's hand will produce little effect. If A relaxes his left arm, and sends his Ki through it, then when he strikes B's forearm down suddenly, B will feel brief but jarring pain, like that of an electric shock. Then B's Ki will be momentarily cut.

A can do the same thing when B tries to kick him. If A strikes down just as B's foot is about to touch him, he will be able to strike somewhere around B's ankle. The leg feels more pain than the hand. If A strikes B with his arm relaxed and Ki extended, he will effectively discourage B from kicking again.

When A strikes down with his hand, if he brings his arm down right in front of him without moving his shoulders, his hand goes up in a reflex action, and he will be ready for the next attack. This means that A loses nothing should he fail to strike B's hand because he pulls back his hand instantaneously. On the other hand it will be dangerous if A aims for B's hand and tries to strike it forcefully, because he will lose his balance if he misses the hand. A will never lose his balance if he concentrates simply on defending himself rather than on hitting B.

IRIMI-ATE

Again instead of saying, "Yes!", A stands in the left hanmi, and swings his left fist up from below, thrusting it into B's right side when he attacks. This is called IRIMI-ATE because the thrust to the body, which is called ATEMI in Japanese, is performed with the IRIMI method. In applying this technique, A's fist will hit straight into B's side but B's right hand will no more than graze A's chest. However if A tries to thrust at B after blocking or warding off B's hand, B can counterattack with his next move. But if A does not concern himself with B's fist and simply drives his left fist into B's side the moment he attacks, B will have no way to defend himself (photo 106).

106

Why is it that A's fist reaches B's side before B's right hand reaches A, despite the fact that B makes the first move to strike A, and A starts moving only after that? The reason is as follows.

B's fist comes straight to A. A's left arm hangs down at his side and is unbendable because he extends Ki through it. In IRIMI-ATE A swings his left, unbendable arm right at B, without bending it. But if A is not extending Ki through his left arm, he will be unable to hit B effectively. Without Ki he would have to bend his arm once to generate enough power before striking B. If A does this, he will be one move behind B who will now be able to strike him first.

If A extends Ki and correctly hits B with his left arm extended straight out, in the left hanmi, his posture will be turned farther to the right. This movement will naturally move A out of the line of B's attack, making B's fist graze A's chest harmlessly. Moreover since A performs IRIMI-ATE with his Ki fully extended, B's Ki will be thrust aside, and A will be unharmed.

Next instead of saying, "Yes!", A turns his hips to the right. B's fist will pass by A's body after he has moved. Though B may sometimes notice A's movement, once his Ki has moved he cannot change its direction. His movement is like an arrow which once released from the bow cannot change its direction in mid-flight. Thus once A has mastered the timing of "Yes!", no matter how quickly B strikes, he will have ample time to turn his body aside and avoid the attack.

Now let A practice grasping and leading B's right hand when B attacks him. A must not grab B's hand in such a way that he collides with the flow of his force. If he does, it will be like damming up a running river, and all of B's force will come upon A. For once B feels he is stopped, even if A holds his right hand, B can and will attack with his left hand or his legs. However if instead of stopping B's right hand, A lets it go and leads it in the direction dictated by its momentum, B will not be able to attack A. His left hand will go backwards as his body lunges forward. Also as he loses his balance, he will be unable to kick A. It follows, then, that A must catch B's right hand in such a way that he will lead his Ki in the same direction as his thrust.

Standing in right hanmi, B thrusts his right hand forward. Standing on B's right side, A makes a circle with the thumb, the ring finger, and the little finger of his left hand. He moves his hand along B's right arm, from the upper arm down to the wrist. His hand will naturally catch B's wrist as the fist is wider than the wrist. Without stopping there, A leads B's right arm forward in the direction in which his hand is pointing. By leading him in this way, A can make B stumble forward (photo 107).

If A tries to hold B's hand by using his thumb, index, and middle finger for the circle, his hand will surely slip and fail to hold B's hand. If he tenses these fingers, his force will go to his shoulder causing him to lose one point. Also the weight of his arm will rise making it impossible to hold B's hand securely. On the other hand if A uses his thumb, ring and little finger, his weight will remain underside. He will have a strong center to proceed from and will be able to make B stagger forward by stretching his foream the moment his fingers grasp his wrist.

107

Next practice bending the wrist in the KOTEGAESHI throw.

B strongly clenches his fist and thrusts it forward. Holding the wrist with his left thumb, ring, and little fingers, A also uses his right hand in an effort to bend B's fist over and apply KOTE-GAESHI. Since B's force is focused in the center of his wrist when he clenches it powerfully, his Ki flows through the wrist. Thus A will be unable to bend it through sheer force alone.

B's Ki is rolled in and flows along the fingers of his fist. A must follow this Ki direction if he is to throw B. A holds B's wrist with the thumb, ring, and little finger as if to stretch it lightly. Then lightly placing the middle finger of his right hand on the knuckle joint of the middle finger of B's right hand, he slides his middle finger along B's middle finger. In doing so he forces B's finger to curl further into his fist and then thrusts his wrist down, continuing to follow the direction of the fingers. Since A follows the direction of the flow of B's Ki, he cannot resist. His wrist bends, and he falls. If A does not understand this principle, he will not be able to apply the technique of KOTEGAESHI effectively on a strong opponent.

After A has practiced the above exercises well, he may practice the movements in a continuous, fluid sequence. The moment B's Ki reaches A's chest when he comes to strike, A should pivot his hips to the right with the "Yes!" timing. At the same time he should catch B's wrist and lead him around in a circular movement to the right. As B moves around A, A should apply KOTEGAESHI just as B passes in front of him.

Even if B strikes at A's face or other parts of his body. A can throw him using the same technique. Instead of trying to grab B's wrist directly, A has practiced catching B's wrist by sliding his hand down from B's shoulder and along his arm so that it naturally catches at the wrist. Though B can freely move his fist up or down, he cannot move his shoulder so freely and easily. Therefore it is easier for A to catch B's wrist by moving his hand from the relatively stationary shoulder down along the arm. Even if B tries to strike A's face with his fist, A can slide his hand up and grab B's wrist, or down if B punches for A's stomach. In each case by starting from the shoulder and following the arm, A can apply KOTEGAESHI. In any case A is out of danger since he has pivoted out of B's line of attack.

Though there are various defense movements and methods to use against the hands and legs of an opponent's attack, what is essential to them all is training oneself to detect the movement of the opponent's Ki. If one reacts only after he sees his opponent's hand or feet move, he will be too late. Self-defense is only possible by detecting an opponent's intention or Ki. Inability to detect Ki is inability to defend. Just as a pond's turbulent, rough surface cannot reflect objects clearly, the agitated spirit, disturbed by the movement of an opponent's hand or leg, cannot perceive his true intent or Ki movement.

Always strive to keep one point, to create MA-AI, and to intuitively perceive an opponent's intention. Moreover, if one controls the opponent's Ki with one's own strong Ki, there will be no danger or reason to fear.

16. YOKOMENUCHI SHIHO-NAGE IRIMI

Standing in left hanmi, A exposes the left side of his face to B so that it appears that he could hit it easily. B steps towards A with his right foot and strikes at the left side of A's face or neck with his right hand (photo 108).

When B attacks, with his left hand raised and its palm slightly turned towards B, A takes a large step back on toes of his left foot (photo 109).

A directs B's right hand which is coming to hit him, downward by leading the inner side of B's right wrist in his left hand. At the same time he brings his right hand to his left hand and feels as if he envelops B's right hand with his Ki. A must not grab B's hand tightly. Simultaneously A draws his right foot back to his left foot. From this position it will be easy to perform the next movement which will cause B to lose his balance completely (photo 110).

108

109

110

111

A then continues the movement by
swinging B's arm up as he steps forward with his right foot. After swinging
B's arm up, A steps forward with his left
foot placing his toes lightly between B's
feet (photo 111).

Now if A turns his hips completely to
the right, B will fall back with his right
arm over his body (photo 112, 113).

112

113

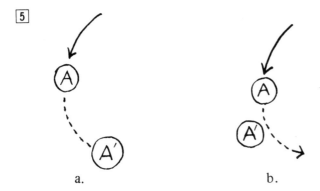

a.   b.

In figure a when B attacks A, A must not move in the same line in which B's right hand is moving. This line is shown by the dotted line in the figure. Since the hand moves more quickly than the body, A will receive B's force if he moves this way. And if B is stronger than A, A will be staggered and unable to perform SHIHO NAGE.

However when A is outside the line of B's force as in figure b, it will not matter how strong B's force is. Leaving only his hand on the dotted line, A can easily catch B's hand as if he were catching a ball and throw him with SHIHO NAGE. The following will explain how to move outside of B's line of attack.

When moving backwards it is very important to draw the right foot back to the left foot. In photo 110 if A does not draw his right foot back and remains holding B's hand in that position, B can either hit A with his left hand or kick him with his left foot. But by drawing his right foot back, A stretches B's right arm out fully and pulls him slightly off balance. Then when B tries to hit or kick with his left hand or foot, A can defend himself easily by slightly moving B's right hand with his right hand and causing him to lose his balance. Remember that whether A will be able to defend himself or not depends on whether he draws his right foot back to his left foot or not.

When B attacks A with a strike to the side, A can generally avoid B's force by taking a large step to the rear with his left foot while continuing to extend Ki forward. But if B were a huge man with a long arm attacking A with all his strength, A may be unable to move outside the line of his attack by merely stepping back on his left foot. Practice the following movements to learn how to move when attacked by such an opponent.

A stands in left hanmi and raises his left knee and waits for the "One"(photo 114).

At the count of "One" keeping his left knee raised, A hops lightly back on his right foot.

At the count of "Two" A steps back as far as possible on the toes of his left foot (photo 115).

At the count of "Three" A shifts his weight to his left foot and at the same time draws back his right foot to his left foot (photo 116).

A should not stagger back when B pushes against his shoulders from the front. Remember that Ki must be continually pouring forward even when the body retreats. After mastering these movements, practice doing all of them in one continuous motion.

Perform the sequence of movements on the count of "One." Then return to the former position but stand in right hanmi this time. Now practice this same exercise from the right hanmi position at the count of "Two." Practice these movements many times to the counts of "One" and "Two," and remember to extend Ki forward all the time. Do not jump awkwardly when moving back. When retreating, move quickly and smoothly while keeping one point.

116   115   114

Skill in this exercise will result in skill in leading the attacker's force no matter how big or strong he may be. Holding B with his Ki, A can control him freely with this skill. And just as the willow tree bends following the force of the wind, A will naturally take a small step back if B's attack is weak, and he will move far back if B's attack is strong.

Standing straight in right hanmi, B keeping one point, extends his right hand forward. This is a very powerful and strong posture. A holds his extended hand firmly with both his hands and tries to throw B down with the SHIHO NAGE technique.

If B starts to lose his posture, A may have a chance to throw him. But as long as his mind and body are unified, that is, as long as he keeps one point, B will be immovable. A will not be able to move B's right hand much less swing it up. Thus some people think that Aikido is not effective on strong people.

Next with both hands A holds B's right wrist very lightly, almost without touching his wrist. Then if he swings B's right hand up to his left in one Ki movement, he will be able to raise B's right hand easily. As long as he does not try to push B's hand back toward him, he will succeed in moving it.

Though A can swing B's right hand up, to lift it past its natural stopping point and to hold it up will be very difficult as his force will collide with B's. Thus almost simultaneously and without over-extending B's arm, A steps in front and across B on his left foot.

At the same time he pivots on the balls of his feet and turns his hips powerfully to the right. B will fall naturally when this SHIHO-NAGE technique is applied. If B does not fall, it means that A has not turned his hips sufficiently. He must turn them until B falls. If A does not forcefully hold up or push down B's tensed right hand, but instead holds it with Ki, concentrates on the image of a circle, and turns his hips quickly to the right, B will fall without offering any resistance.

In the next exercise practice how A throws B in SHIHO NAGE by lowering his right hand. Unless the principle of Ki is understood, it will not be clear why A can throw B by making a complete turn with his hips.

B bends his right arm and places it in the position it would be when he is thrown with SHIHO NAGE. Then he keeps weight under-side so that the weight of his arm settles in the elbow's lowest

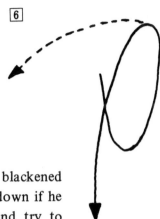

6

point. Moreover he holds his elbow down with his left hand to stop his right arm from going up.

A tries to lower B's arm with the SHIHO NAGE throw. If A tries to throw him in the direction of the dotted arrow by trying to raise B's right elbow, he will find it impossible. Thus in failing to raise B's elbow, A fails to throw him down.

In this instance B's Ki moves in the direction of the blackened arrow and not the dotted arrow. Many fail to throw B down if he is strong because they misperceive his Ki movement and try to throw him in the direction of the dotted arrow. But remember to throw someone it is necessary to move and lead the mind since it is the mind that moves the body. Thus in this case A must throw B in the direction of the blackened arrow since his Ki is directed that way. If A simultaneously drops his right hand (with which he holds B's right hand) and with his left hand strokes the back of B's right hand straight down, B will fall without any resistance. There is no reason to hold B's hand up while trying to throw him backwards. All that A has to do is drop his hands naturally, and B's hand will follow.

Following the momentum generated by swinging his arms up and to the right, A should turn his hips completely to the right. If he does this, both arms will pass over his head and come down naturally as shown by the arrow in the diagram.

This arrow portrays the movement of A's Ki when he throws B with SHIHONAGE. When A grips B's right hand, steps across with his left foot, and twists his hips only slightly to the right, B's hand will still be high up. If A tries to force his hand down by pressing it against his shoulder, he must be careful not to hurt B's arm which will be forced into an unnatural position. Moreover because it feels wrong, B will resist A's attempt to throw him. This unnatural movement is unnecessary.

If A turns his hips farther to the right, B's wrist will naturally come down while the elbow of his bent arm will go up, and B will lose his balance. If A turns his hips farther to the right, both hands will fall naturally. Since in this case, B's arm, hand, and wrist is bent in the direction it naturally bends, this technique does not work contrary to natural laws. It is in the order of the natural.

TENKAN

When B attacks with a strike to the side of A's head, A moves outside of B's attack and catches his right hand. From there moving in to the right of B, A turns clockwise to throw B with the tenkan method of SHIHO-NAGE.

When A moves in to the right of B, A should not hold B's hand strongly or push it toward B's shoulder. The weight of B's right arm is underside. So if A collides against B's power, A will not be able to move B's hand. A must hold B's hand lightly with Ki and extend Ki in the same direction as B using the Five Principles of Shin-Shin Toitsu Aikido. B will follow A gladly.

Since Aikido uses many techniques involving an opponent's joints in throwing an opponent, many think that Aikido uses harmful, unnatural techniques. But this is a mistaken conception. There are both unnatural and natural joint techniques. Those that bend joints in the way they naturally bend are called jun. Those that bend joints forcefully in an unnatural way are called gyaku.

In Aikido, whether the throw be SHIHONAGE, KOTEGAESHI, NIKYO, or others which will be explained later, only jun techniques are used. Joints are bent in their normal, natural directions. Caught by the jun techniques, the opponent cannot resist and is thrown, but will not be hurt. If an opponent should be hurt, it reveals that there was not sufficient training in the correct application of the throw, and that not jun but unnatural force was used instead. Just being able to throw another is not sufficient. Simply throwing someone does not mean one has correctly mastered the throw or understood the principles behind it. To do this one must always train with close attention to each movement, always following "the natural" in all things.

What is in harmony with Nature is in order, is natural. What is against the unifying harmony of Nature is out of order, is unnatural. To use unnatural techniques in a discipline such as Aikido which strives for the unification of ourselves with the principles of

118

119

Nature is completely wrong.

If we practice the unnatural, our spirits will become perverted one day. Consequently we will think that the end justifies the means, and that anything is permissible in order to win over another. Finally this view may culminate in the compassionless spirit that equates justice with brute power and that considers the weak as destined to be the natural victims of the strong.

We must always practice that justice is power, and not that power is justice. If we practice the natural, we can naturally extend Ki. If each teacher extends Ki strongly, all the pupils will follow him gladly.

120

121

17. SHOMENUCHI KOKYUNAGE

A stands in right hanmi. Swinging his right hand up, B strikes straight down with it, aiming for the middle of A's forehead (photo 122).

The moment B comes to strike A's forehead, A swings his right hand up along his side. He extends Ki strongly through his arm and directs it to the other side of B's right hand. Then B's force will not strike A's forehead. Instead his Ki will be deflected to the outside of A's arm by A's own strong flow of Ki. Consequently his arm will pass harmlessly by A's right side and strikes the floor rather than his head (photo 123).

Just as A leads B's arm by him, he steps behind B on his right side by taking a step forward on his left foot. At the same time, as B's right arm slides on the outside of his, A lowers it further with his own right arm. Also A holds B's neck with his left hand.

A steps even father behind B by pivoting his body to the right and stepping back with his right foot. A must harmonize the force of his forward movement with that of B's attack; then B will naturally be led downwards in a circle around A's right side (photo 124).

122   123

B's reaction will be to raise his lowered head in an effort to regain his balance. Using the upward force B exerts, A leads B further up than he expects by swinging his right hand up fully. Then when A straightens himself up, B will end up facing upwards, and his body bent backward (photo 125).

A turns his right hand in a circle so that his index finger points toward B and then drops his hand as if to thrust his finger right between B's eyes. But just before hitting his face, if A instead thrusts his index finger down past B's left cheek, B will fall backwards (photo 126).

124

125

126

When B tried to strike A with a downward blow to the forehead, A swang his right arm up and by extendi   Ki was ble to lead the force of B's blow past him and to the floor. He did not try to block or stop the strike. Skill in doing this is important. If the art of leading the blow is mastered, B will be easy to manage no matter how strong he may be. Practice this in the following example.

Standing in right hanmi, A is attacked by B who strikes at his forehead with a downward blow from his right hand. If B strikes down with the weight of his arm on the underside, his blow will be very powerful. A receives his blow by shielding his forehead with his right arm. A will be able to do this only as long as his arm is stronger than B's. But if B is stronger than him, A will be struck down by him despite his attempt to block. Consequently he will be unable to step behind B's right to throw him with SHOMEN-UCHI KOKYUNAGE.

If A calms his spirit by concentrating himself at his one point and extends Ki strongly through his right arm, his arm will be immovable. When B attacks if he swings this unbendable arm up naturally. B's right hand will not even hit his arm but will head for the floor to his right. To understand the principles involved here, the following example may help.

Picture water gushing strongly out of a fire hose. Water from another hose cannot be made to flow towards the mouth of that hose. Of course if the force of water from the fire hose is weak and that of the other water much stronger, then the water from the second hose can reach the fire hose. But as long as the force of water from the fire hose is strong and steady, there is no need to worry about other water. Since A pours forth strong Ki through his right hand, B's force is turned aside just as water aimed at a gushing fire hose is also deflected and does not reach the mouth of the hose. Of course if he is to succeed, A must do this exercise with absolute confidence.

Next let us examine how A leads B's body down after he leaps behind his right side.

Standing in right hanmi, B extends a strongly tensed right arm with its fist clenched. B stands firm, determined not to allow A to strike his arm down. A gives B's upper arm a strong blow. If A and B are equal in strength, A will be unable to strike B's right arm down (photo 127).

Fully relaxing his raised right arm, A lays it gently on B's right upper arm, so gently that he is hardly aware of it. Then if A keeps the weight of his arm underside and lowers his right hand naturally, he will be able to bring B's right arm down easily (photo 128).

128

127

The Principle of Nidan-Biki (taking up the slack)

Standing in right hanmi, B holds a towel in his right hand and bends his right arm at a right angle (photo 129).

A holds the other side of the towel in his right hand and pulls it camly. The towel stretches until it naturally stops. This is taking up the slack (photo 130). A should not pull strongly but very softly until this point. From this point A pulls in one motion, B will stagger forward (photo 131).

If A pulls strongly from the beginning, A's power will stop when the slack is taken up and A cannot move B. Similarly in photo 127, if A tenses his right hand from the beginning, his force collids with B's arm and stops. A's Ki stops and he fails to strike down B's arm.

A must bring down his arm and lay it gently on B's arm. This is the equivalent of taking up the slack. From here A lowers his right hand in a relaxed but firm way, and thus is able to effectively lower B's right arm.

The same principle works when A lowers B's neck using his left hand.

131

Before important events many people worry uselessly in anticipation, and when the event actually occurs they are powerless and stupefied. These people should remember and practice the nidanbiki principle. While events are still in the air, they should not fret and tense themselves uselessly. Instead they should relax and calm themselves by keeping one point. Then they will be in a powerful, alert state ready to do their utmost when the actual moment comes. Since ancient days it has been recognized that the greater a man is, the calmer he is when important matters arise.

EXERCISE

A stands in right hanmi. At the command of "One", he swings up both hands as he steps forward with his left foot. He continues pivoting around his left foot 180 degrees as his arms swing down and then up to the right side with centrifugal force. The right hand stops above the head and the left hand at the right arm pit. It is a mixture of UDEMAWASHI UNDO and UDEFURI CHOYAKU UNDO. A's right hand should be immovable when B tries to push it down. Repeat this exercise on both sides.

132

133

Third Level

18. FUNEKOGI UNDO

A stands in left hanmi. At the count of "One," A thrusts his hips slightly forward, and with his wrists bent naturally, raise both wrists and thrusts them straight forward. A should not lean his upper body forward, backward, right or left. The weight of the upper body should be in the one point. The rear leg should be stretched out comfortably (photo 132).

At the count of "Two", A pulls his hips backward, and brings both hands in to his waist. The rear leg is bent slightly and the forward leg is stretched out (photo 133).

When A thrusts out his hands, B pushes A's hands towards his shoulders. A's hands should not move back. If A keeps one point and extends Ki from the arms, A should be immovable.

Next when A brings his hands in to his waist, B stands in front of A and pushes A's shoulders. A should not move backward. B can also test A by pushing his wrists towards his shoulders. If the weight of A's arms is underside, they should not move.

A repeats this exercise with left foot forward and then right foot forward.

It is rather easy to unify mind and body when one is not moving. It is more difficult to maintain the one point in motion. One must practice to move from his one point in every day activities.

When A's hands are outstretched, B seizes A's hand (photo 134). If A tries to pull his hands in toward his hips, he will encounter B's strength and be stopped. A should pull his hips in without moving his hands until B's arms are stretched out to their full extent (photo 135). Then A can easily pull his hands and B will move forward off balance (photo 136)

19. NIKYO UNDO

If an arm may be compared to a fire hose, the wrist is like the nozzle on the hose. The nozzle is useless for shooting out water to extinguish fires unless it is strong and easily directed. Similarly if a person is to be able to freely pour out strong Ki and guide his opponent's Ki at will in Aikido, he must train his wrists so they are strong, supple, and flexible.

A bends his left wrist outward. Then placing his right palm over the back of his left hand, A pushes his left upper arm and elbow toward the palm of his right hand. Simultaneously he takes up any slack in his left wrist by bending it slightly with his right hand (photo 137). The combined force on his left wrist, will stretch the muscles of his wrist well. Done correctly, this exercise will naturally stretch a cord which runs from the wrist to the base of the neck. It prevents and cures stiff shoulders and high blood pressure.

In doing this exercise A's Ki should flow out through his left hand as in figure a. This is extending Ki.

A's Ki must not flow back to him as in the figure b. If this happens the exercise is meaningless. Try this exercise four times on each side.

137

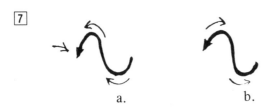

a.   b.

20. KOTEGAESHI UNDO

As in photo 138 A bends his left wrist palm up. He holds his left wrist with his right hand by catching the little finger and ring finger of his right hand on his left wrist joint. His right thumb should be placed in the back of his left ring finger. Then A twists his left wrist as much as he can. But in twisting it he should not push the wrist only with the thumb of his right hand. If he does this, all his force will back up into his right shoulder. Instead, thinking he holds it with Ki, A should grasp his left wrist lightly but firmly with his right hand. Then A should simply lower both hands. Force will naturally flow into his thumb, and his left wrist will twist well at the joint. Try this exercise four times on each side.

138

100

21. SANKYO UNDO

A turns his left hand so that his palm faces outward and the little finger side of his hand is up. He wraps the four fingers of his right hand around the side of his left little finger and places his right thumb behind his left thumb.

Then A thrusts out both hands rhythmically.

Repeat this four times with each hand. Doing this exercise will stretch the chords on the little finger side of the hand well.

When A thrusts out both hands, B pushes them towards A's shoulders. If A's arms are tense or too much stretched, A will lose balance. If A relaxes his arms completely, there is a place where his hands naturally stop. If A's hands stop there calmly, A will not move when pushed by B (photo 140).

139

140

22. KATATORI NIKYO

IRIMI

The beginning of this throw is the same as in KATATORI IKKYO. B attempts to grab A's left shoulder. A steps back on his left foot and leads B's right hand down lightly with his right hand. Then he swings it in an arc up and towards B's face and down. He also steps forward on his left foot (photo 144).

After having had his arm swung down, A brings B's right arm up with his left hand and brings the back of B's right hand to his left shoulder with his own right hand.

A lightly grips B's right wrist with his left hand. As he does so, he should twist the wrist as if he were rolling it inward from the outer side (photo 145). Then with both hands he bends B's right hand downward. B will feel sharp pain in his right wrist and fall quickly to the ground (photo 146).

A then removes his left hand from B's right wrist and places it on B's right upper arm. Then pushing B down, he holds him with his face down. A holds B's right hand as shown in photo 147. Then holding it from the outer side with his left hand, A should turn it downwards.

141

142

143

144

145

146

147

103

148

149

TENKAN

After A swings B's right hand in his direction, A jumps well behind B (photo 151). A puts his left hand on his right elbow and leads B around and down (photo 152). Next he brings B's right wrist to his left shoulder with the feeling of scooping his entire body up (photo 153).

A then applies NIKYO and pins B down (photo 154, 155, 156)

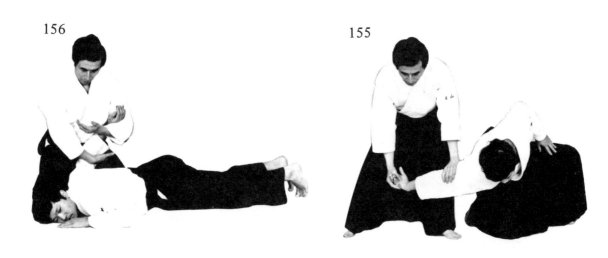

156

155

150

151

152

153

154

23. KATATORI SANKYO

The beginning of this throw is the same as in KATATORI NIKYO.

IRIMI

A swings B's right hand up and down, and once B is bent down and unable to rise, A releases his elbow and with his left hand grips B's right hand from the side of his little finger (photo 161). He then takes the underside(now turned up) of his elbow in the right hand (photo 162) and leads B's arm around and down.

Once B is down, A takes B's hand, from the little finger side in his right hand and B's elbow in his left. A then bends B's arm till the pain makes him give in (photo 163, 164).

TENKAN

A leads B's hand down and swings it up. Then A jumps behind B and continues turning as he brings down B's arm. He then takes a SANKYO hold in the same way as IRIMI and pins B down.

At this point, I want to caution you about techniques that involve bending joints. Remember that in Aikido we always bend the joint in the natural direction; to force it the wrong way would be to violate the laws of the universal. Properly executed, Aikido techniques never injure the body, but are good for health. They stretch the joint at the instant of application, then causing pain, but once the pressure is released, the stretched joint feels light and relaxed.

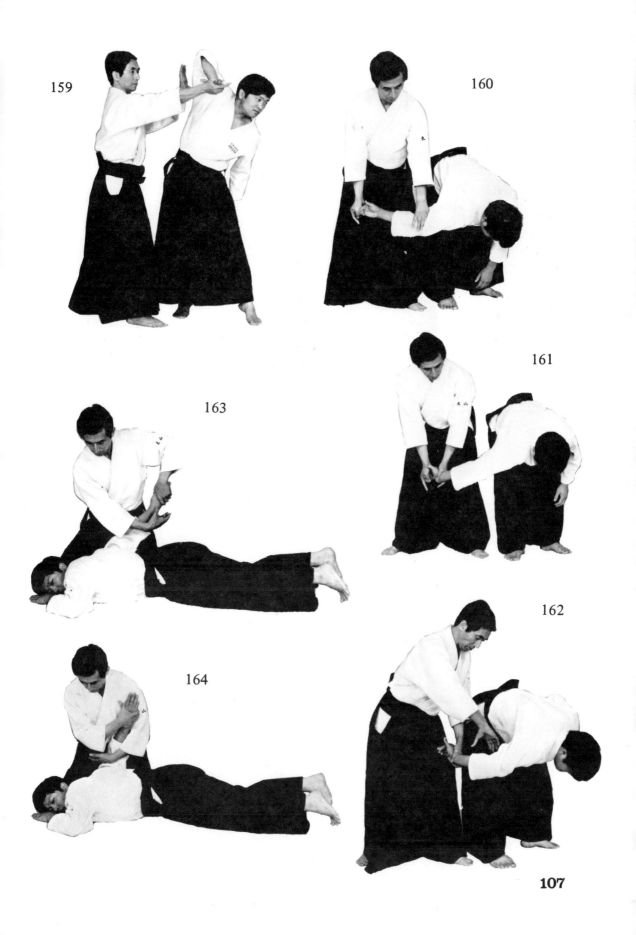

159

160

161

162

163

164

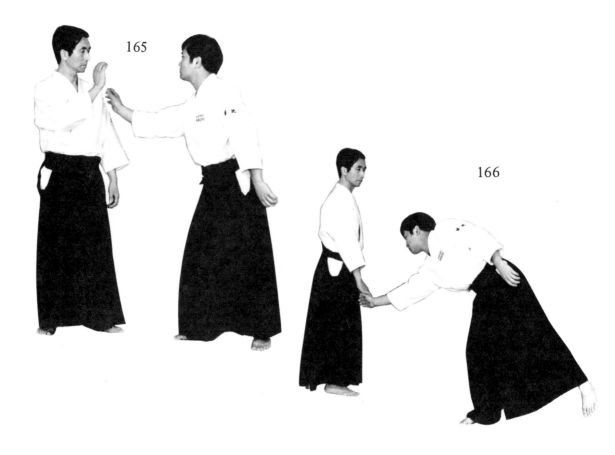

165

166

24. KATATORI YONKYO

IRIMI

A begins as in KATATORI SANKYO. A moves his left hand to
B's forearm and then his right hand to B's wrist (photo 169). He
concentrates his Ki in the lower knuckle of his left index finger,
applying pressure to the bone in the forearm near the base of the
thumb. B will follow in a parabolic line leading to A's right foot and
then fall (photo 170). If A uses the base of his left index finger
properly, B will feel a sharp pain and follow where A leads.

TENKAN

A jumps behind B and applies YONKYO in the same way as IRIMI.
When A changes his grip, he must be careful not to cut his Ki movement.

To pin him down, A keeps his grip on B's wrist and gives more
pressure. B will feel a sharp pain.

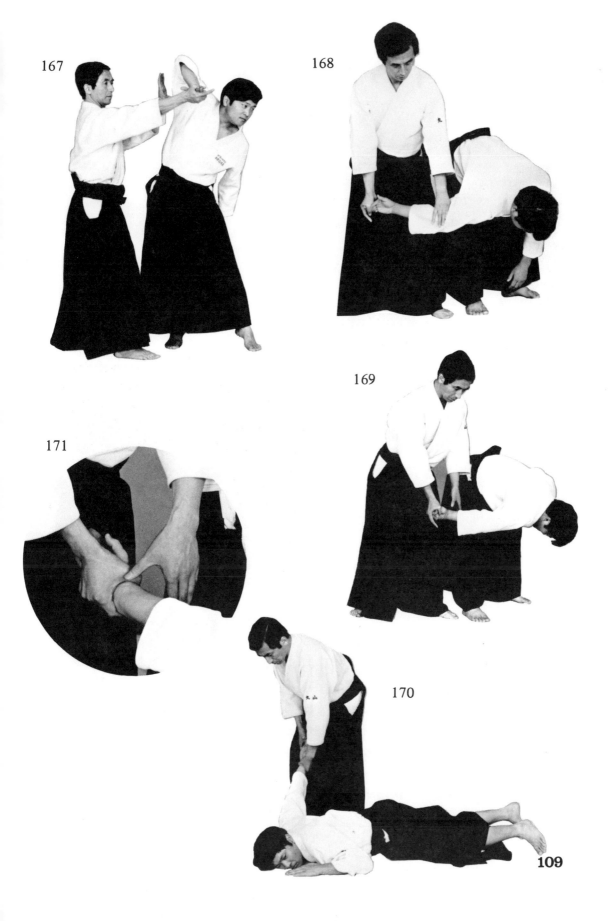

167

168

169

171

170

109

172

173

25. YOKOMENUCHI KOKYU NAGE (1)

A stands in left hanmi. B tries to strike the left side of A's face with his right hand (photo 172).

A steps back on his left foot as he extends Ki towards B and swings both arms up in a relaxed way (photo 173).

A hits down B's arm with his left hand and the left side of B's neck with his right hand. B will fall down (photo 174).

A should not really hit B's neck. Instead A extends Ki towards B so that B's Ki moves.

174

175 176

26. RYOTETORI KOKYUNAGE

B, in left hanmi, grips both of A's hands (photo 175).

Without altering the positions of his wrists, A steps as far to the rear as possible on his left foot, putting only the toes on the floor (photo 176).

The instant the toes of his left foot touch the floor, A turns his face and body to his left. As A shifts his weight to the left, B will naturally fall off balance to the front (photo 177).

A throws B's right hand down. B will somersault and fall (photo 178).

If B is keeping one point, it is difficult to lead him forward. A must practise FUNEKOGI UNDO well.

B stands in right hanmi with his right hand outstretched. A holds his right wrist with his right hand and tries to throw B by thrusting the hand down (photo 179).

If B's arm is loose and relaxed, A merely lowers it and this has no effect on B (photo 180). But if A first pulls B's arm taut and then thrusts it down, B will somesault and fall (photo 181).

After A has mastered this movement, A steps back when B moves in to seize both A's hands. When B's arms are fully outstretched, A takes his right wrist from underside. When B's body is led upward, A thrusts his right hand down. B will fall.

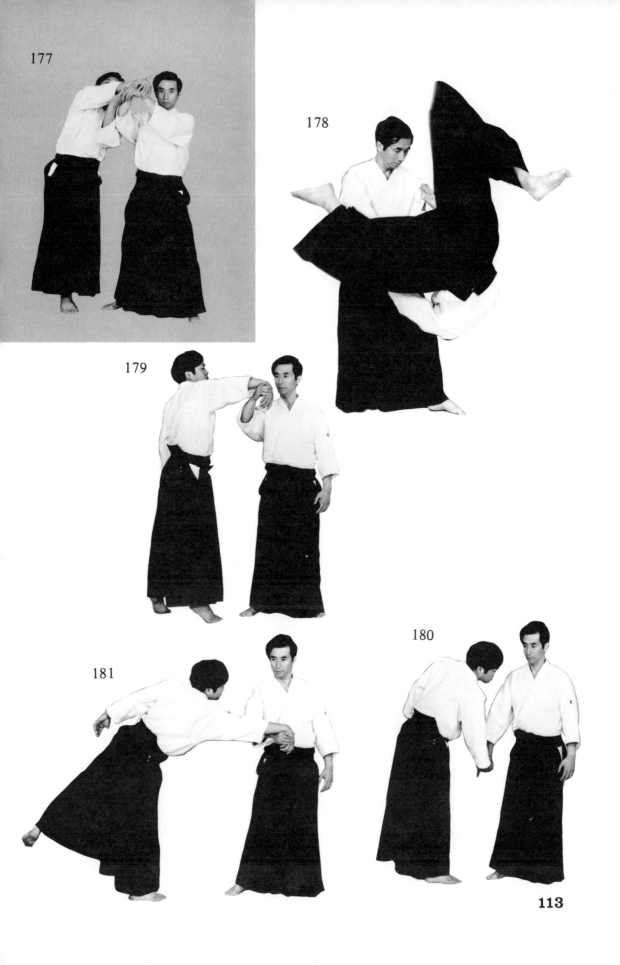

177

178

179

181

180

113

FOURTH LEVEL

27. TEKUBI KOSA UNDO

A stands facing forward with both arms hanging relaxed. On the count of "One", A bends both wrists and crosses them in front of his body (photo 182) and then lets them separate naturally (photo 183). He continues to repeat the exercise four times with the right hand outside and then four times with the left hand outside. During this exercise even if B tells him to stop when his hands are crossed and pushes his wrists up, A should not let his hands come up nor let his body sway back. If he relaxes both arms and keeps weight underside in his hands, his hands will naturally stay down. If the weight is upperside, that is, on the side of his upturned palms or if his shoulders are tensed, A's hands will be pushed up or his body will sway back when tested by B.

182   183

184

185

Letting B grasp both his wrists with all his strength, A tries to do this exercise of crossing his wrists (photo 184). If A tenses his wrists, he will not be able to move since they will collide with B's force. But if A relaxes his arms and hands completely, keeps weight under-side, and moves from his fingertips, he will be able to move them easily, no matter how hard B may try to stop him (photo 185).

The same thing applies to daily life. Most people put strength when they encounter difficulties. Thus they get tense and lose power. If they keep one point and relax, they can easily deal with most difficulties.

186

Next A swings up both hands to eye level (photo 186).

A should not move when B attempts to push his hands toward him (photo 187).

If A stops his Ki or puts strength in his shoulders or arms, he will easily move.

A must keep one point and relax his arms when he swings up his hands. Then his power is flowing centrifugally, that is toward the back of his hands.

187

188

28. USHIROTORI UNDO

So far B has always attacked from the front. However A should be able to deal with attacks from behind as well.

Before practising the techniques for attacks from behind, lets practise several exercises.

Standing with his legs apart, A lets both his arms hang down and turns the arms and palms outward as much as he can (photo 188).

At the count of "One," A turns his arms inwards, spreading them to form the sides of an isosceles triangle, and simultaneously takes a step forward on his left foot. His fingers must be straight and pointed in the direction his arms are extended (photo 189).

At the count of "Two," bending his left knee and stretching his right leg naturally, A leans the upper part of his body forward. His left hand should be pointed down to the front; his right hand should be swung fully to the back. His face should be turned to the front (photo 190). Riding on the reaction to this movement, A returns to the standing posture just as a ball thrown down bounces up.

At the counts of "Three" and "Four," he steps out on his right foot and repeats the same movements described above on the opposite side.

189

190

A stands and spreads his arms like the sides of an isosceles triangle. Holding A's upper arms with both hands, B tries to force A's extended arms to collapse by pushing in on them. But if A keeps one point, relaxes, and extends Ki, he will be able to keep his arms extended with perfect ease. No matter how hard he may try, B will not be able to force A's arms in (photo 191).

On the other hand, if A tenses both arms, B will be able to force them in easily.

When A places his left foot forward, swings his left hand down, his right hand up, and leans the upper part of his body forward, he must remain immovable even if his arms or hips are pushed from behind (photo 192).

He can do this if he turns his face to the front, calms himself by keeping one point, and completely relaxes his arms and legs.

A stands in right hanmi and stretches his right arm out. First A makes a ring with his thumb and the index finger and puts strength there. B pushes A's right hand toward his shoulder. A will receive B's power to his shoulder and move.

Next A bends the small finger and the ring finger. Then all B's power is absorbed in A's one point and A will not move. In this way the line of the small finger is connected to the one point. When A turns this line out, B cannot force A's arms in.

191

192

29. USHIRO TEKUBITORI ZENSHIN UNDO

A stands naturally and lets his arms hang with both wrists bent and the fingers pointing upward (photo 193).

At the count of "One", he swings both hands up over his head as he takes a step forward on his left foot (photo 195).

At the count of "Two", he bends his left knee, leaving his right knee stretched, and bends his body forward. He also swings both arms downward to the front (photo 196). He returns to the original position and repeats the exercise beginning on the right foot.

In the position of photo 193, should B push A's hands upward, A's arms must not bend and A's body must be immovable. If A is keeping one point, the weight of the arms is in the lowest part.

In the position of photo 195, B tries to push down A's hands. If A keeps one point and relaxes, B's push should have no effect. In the position of photo 196, B's push from behind should not move A. B can also test A by pushing his hands towards his shoulders. If A keeps one point and relaxes, he will be immovable.

30. USHIRO TEKUBITORI KOSHIN UNDO

A stands naturally with his wrists bent (photo 197).

At the count of "One", he swings up both hands and takes a half step backward on his left foot (photo 198) then he reverses the direction of his hands so that his fingers are forward (photo 199).

At the count of "Two", he takes a large step to the rear on his right foot, and lowers his arms and upper body (photo 220).

He returns to the original position and repeats the exercise beginning on the right foot. B can test A in the same way as USHIRO TEKUBITORI ZENSHIN UNDO. When retreating, one tends to withdraw one's Ki. One must extend Ki stronger when one retreats.

195

196

197

198

194

193

199

200

121

31. USHIRO TEKUBITORI KOKYUNAGE

A stands naturally and B takes hold of both wrists from behind. Relaxing his arms completely, A bends his hands up (photo 201).

Since A's fingertips are turned upward, both A's Ki and B's Ki are moving upward. A raises his hands as if scratching his head. B's hands will easily follow (photo 202). A points his finger tips forward, keeping his wrists bent and takes a step forward on his left foot (photo 203).

Leading B's Ki forward, A lowers his arms and head. B will roll over A's body and down (photo 204).

When B holds A's hands, if A withdraws his Ki backward, his mind and body are separated. A must keep one point, face forward, and extends Ki forward.

201

202

8

When B holds A's hands, A bends his hands so that his fingertips are turned upward. Both A and B's Ki are moving in the direction of the arrow (fig. 8).

If the arm is the firehose, the fingertips are the nozzle. If he raises his hands from his fingertips, A can lead B's power upward easily. Without directing B's Ki, it would be impossible to raise the hands.

When A swings up his hands and points his fingers forward, if he pushes his hands forward, B's hands will fall apart. A must bend his wrists well and lead B's Ki and hands all the time.

If A wants to throw B on his left side, A must step forward on his left foot so that the left hand is thrust out a bit more forward than the right.

204

203

32. USHIRO TEKUBITORI KUBISHIME SANKYO NAGE

Standing behind A, B attempts to strangle him with his right hand while holding A's left wrist with his left hand.

Fully bending his left wrist inward and thrusting out the back of his hand, A turns his fingers to his right. In the same manner he bends his right wrist and fingers towards the center (photo 205). As he does this he must keep the weight of his hands underside. Crossing his wrists as in TEKUBI-KOSA UNDO, A grabs the fingers of B's left hand in his right hand from below (photo 206).

Just as both hands meet, A raises B's left hand with both arms in a continuous motion until his left hand is at the same level with the upper part of his forehead (photo 207). Since A cannot easily move B's left hand from there, he leaves it there, turns his hips clockwise, and steps to B's left rear with his right foot.

At the same time, A leads B's hand straight down with both hands (photo 208). Then after coming up again A applies a SANKYO lock on B's left wrist and then throws him forward (photo 209, 210).

207

206

205

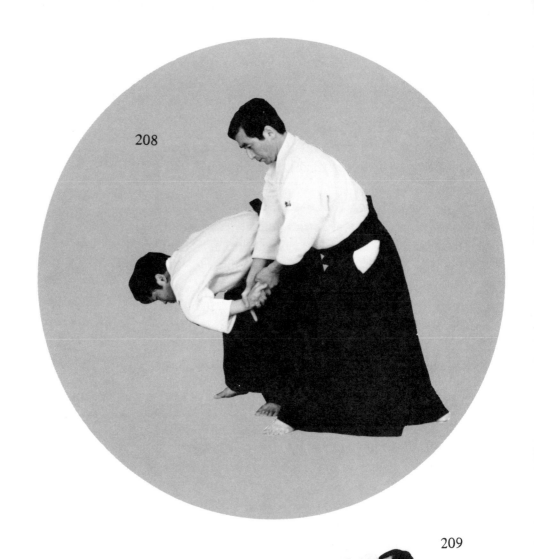

208

210

209

When B tries to strangle A, if A resists keeping his chin inside, B can strangle A's chin and neck together causing A to fall backward.

A must concentrate his mind at his one point in the lower abdomen to absorb B's power. Then B cannot strangle A.

In photo 206 A can move his hands easily if he keeps their weight underside and moves from his fingertips. This is why he can easily reach and hold the fingers of B's left hand in his right hand. Then to raise B's left hand up as in photo 207, A need only practice in such a way that B's left hand rises by the power of A's hands coming together just as foam rises on the crests of two colliding waves. If A misses this timing, B's hand will get very heavy. A will find it difficult to raise in this case.

It is difficult for A to move B's left hand from this position in photo 207 because any further effort will collide against B's force. Up to here it was easy for him to move B's arm, now instead of moving it further, A must change his own body position. After A has moved out, B's hand will be left without any kind of support. So if A thrusts it straight down from that position, B will stagger and lose his balance completely. Consequently he will be unable to kick him or attack him with his right hand.

Now let us proceed to the SANKYO explanation.

Grasping B's left hand in his right hand from the side of his little finger, A twists his hand toward his left shoulder softly and as far as naturally possible. He stops twisting just before it becomes unnatural. B should not feel any pain up to this point. Then A holds B's left fingers in his left hand and twists these to the right towards B's left shoulder. Again he stops twisting before it becomes unnatural (photo 211).

126

But from here, if A pushes B's hands up and towards his shoulder with both his hands even the slightest degree, B will feel sharp pain and jump up. In this position, if B tries to attack A with his free right hand, B will force the SANKYO hold upon himself. Again feeling sharp pain, he will be unable to attack A. Instead B will have to do whatever A wants. This is the best technique for the police to use in making arrests.

211

33. RYOTETORI TENCHI NAGE

IRIMI

B stands in right hanmi and holds both A's wrists. A stands in left hanmi with both arms forward (photo 212).

A lowers his hips slightly and steps deep to B's right rear on his left foot. As A leads B's right hand to his right rear, A lowers his right elbow. Without raising or lowering the hand itself, A turns the fingers of his right hand upward. Both A's hands must always be extending Ki (photo 213).

A then raises his body as he swings up his right hand in the movement described in figure 9 (photo 214).

A raises his right knee, pointing his right fingers toward B's face (photo 215). A lowers his right fingers toward B's face so that it indicates a line skimming the left side of B's face and continuing to the ground. A follows the movement by taking a big step forward to B's right rear on his right foot.

212

213

9

214

215

129

If B maintains his one point and keeps the weight of his hands underside, A will have difficulty using this technique.

B stands in right hanmi with his clenched right fist thrust forward. A pushes against B's fist and tries to move it, first to the right, then to the left. Because A's strength collides with B's, moving B's hand will be difficult. If A pulls B's fist and tries to move it, A will get the same result.

If, on the other hand, A lightly grips B's fist, leads B's Ki forth, and causes B to stretch his arm out a little, A will be able to move B's hand easily (photo 216).

The same thing can be applied in daily life. There are many who upset themselves and get tense over small difficulties. If one is calm, there are very few difficulties in the world.

218

219

B keeps one point in right hanmi and grips A's left hand with his right hand. A stands in left hanmi and relaxes his left hand completely. Relaxing his left hand and keeping weight underside causes B's arm to stretch slightly. A will be able to move it easily. If A tries to drive his left hand to B's right rear, B's strength will stop A. A must relax his hand instead, turning his fingers toward B's rear right. Letting his left side move his left hand, A takes a large step to B's right rear with his left foot and brings his right foot in toward his left (photo 218).

A steps deep to B's right rear with his right foot and gets his shoulder past B's body. B will fall to the rear (photo 219).

Although it is possible to make B fall down with A's left hand only, when A has his right hand around B's neck, he cannot achieve the same effect because in this position he cannot step behind B.

B is standing facing A and is directing all of his Ki backward. To force him down backward, A has to simply put his right arm around B's neck and push down. The backward flow of his Ki makes it easy to move him in that direction. Should he direct his Ki forward, however, A achieves nothing with this approach.

B keeps one point and directs his Ki forward. A tries to push him down in the same manner. A will not only be unable to push B down but also will risk being thrown by B.

When A pushes B's right hand with his left hip and steps forward with his left foot, he crouches and without changing the position of his right wrist, lowers his right elbow, so that the fingers turn upward (photo 221).
Next A rises to his full height and extends his right arm as far up as it will naturally go as if he were supporting the entire heavens with that hand (photo 222).

220

221

222

223

Now he points the fingers of his right hand down toward B's face and raises his right knee (photo 223). A lowers his right hand as if he were going to thrust his fingers into the earth. With this movement A makes B fall down.

A really needs no partner to practise this movement. The important thing is to generate dynamic Ki movement as he rises from the crouching position.

In effect, A leads B's Ki, which was originally directed to the front, downward, upward and then turns it back and downward along B's forehead.

Having studied the movements of each arm, A must now practise them in simultaneous action. When B's hands come to grip A's, A lowers his hips and rises to lead B's Ki and throws B.

TENKAN

A stands in left hanmi and B stands in right hanmi and grips A's hands (photo 224).

A turns the fingers of his right hand up along the inside of B's arm and directs his left hand palm downward as if it were holding down the earth.

Leaving his hands as they are, A takes a step back on his right toes. After A has succeeded in leading B straight forward with the movement of his hips (photo 225), A begins a turn to his right. B is still holding A's hands, so, in keeping with the law of centrigugal force, he must follow A's movement (photo 226). At a suitable point, A stops, lowers his right elbow suddenly, turns the fingers of the right hand up, and crouches. B will lose his balance and fall forward (photo 227).

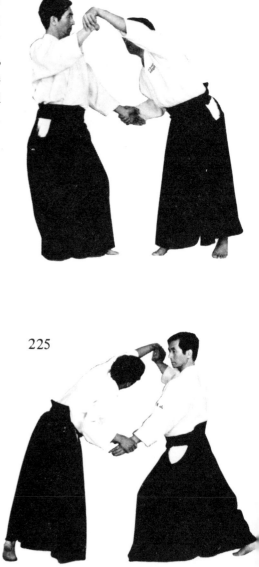

226

224

225

227

228

A rises at once, raise his right hand high and leads B upward (photo 228). If A now turns his fingers towards the ground, B will fall (photo 229).

Once A masters these moves, A will be able to use either the IRIMI or the TENKAN version the moment B tries to grip A's hands.

229

34. USHIROTORI KOKYU NAGE

B grabs A in a bear hug from behind with both his arms. Since B holds him with all his strength, A can neither move forward, nor raise his arms up (photo 230).

Not trying to raise his arms, A keeps both of them hanging straight down and relaxed. Then turning the muscles of his upper arms outward, he thrusts both arms backward while steadily extending his Ki through them (photo 231).

Next A turns the muscles of his upper arms inward from their outward position. The movement of the muscles will lead B's upper arms and his mind forward. As this happens, A will easily be able to raise and spread his arms, thus forcing B upward from the floor. When he leads him up off the floor, A should step forward with his right foot at the same time (photo 232).

Then A leans forward, pointing his right finger to the floor before him, and swings his left hand high up to the rear.

B will slide down and off A's body and fall forward, turning over once (photo 233).

230

231

232

233

The most essential things in this throw are in photo 231 and 232 when A turns his arms outwards and then in. Unless A does this, he will not move his opponent's mind and will be helpless when held by a man of great physical strength. Let A realize and master this principle through the following exercises.

A stands with his right hand held out. B grabs A's right wrist in both hands with all his strength. If A tries to move his right hand forward or backward, to the right or to the left, or up or down, he will find it very difficult since he will collide with B's force.

But in fact A can turn his wrist to the right or to the left without really moving it from where it is held by B. Because there is space between the bone and the skin of A's wrist, and B does not hold the bone, A can certainly turn the bone of his wrist if he relaxes his right hand. However be sure that A relaxes his hand and arm; otherwise he will not be able to turn it.

B grasps A's right upper arm with all his strength. Since there is more space between the bone and skin of the upper arm than between those of the wrist, this time A can turn his upper arm to the right or to the left more easily than before.

So no matter how tightly B may wrap his arms around his upper arms, A can easily turn his arms outwards and then back in as long as he relaxes both arms completely. In turning his upper arms outwards, A tries to spread them and get them as close as possible to B's arms. Thus rubbing his upper arms against the inside of B's, A leads B's arm forward and spreads his own so that they resemble the sides of an isosceles triangle. Unless A catches on to B's upper arms when rubbing them, he will be unable to extend his arms out to the side. When A spreads his arms out, he should be careful not to hit against B's bent forearm, that is, the area between the elbows and the fingers of B's arms. If A does, he will be unable to move because he will then collide with B's force.

A should only lead the parts of B's arms shown in fig. 10 in thick lines. A should stop rubbing his arms forward just before they reach the end of the heavy lines drawn on B's arms and should walk forward keeping this posture. If A goes beyond the end of the lines, he will collid with B's force. If A can walk easily it means he has performed the exercise of leading B correctly.

Next when A steps forward on his right foot in photo 232, he must step straight forward. If he puts his right foot in front of his left foot and twists the upper part of his body to the left, B's body will follow his and slide to the right. B will naturally take a step forward on his right foot. Consequently A will be unable to throw B off to the right from this position since his right foot will now be able to act as a brace. When A steps forward with his right foot, he must step straight out and move the upper part of his body directly forward without turning to the left the least bit. Then B will not be led to step forward on his right foot. Instead the weight of B's body will fall on A's back. The moment this happens, A should lean forward to the right and swing his right hand down and his left hand up towards his back. This will cause B to slip down and off his back as if he were on a slide, and A will succeed in throwing him.

When A throws B, he must always face the direction in which he throws him. If A carelessly turns backwards, he will lose his balance and may fall down together with B.

A thinks too negatively if he thinks that he helplessly is being held down when B grabs him tightly. Instead A should think that he is letting B hold him. In practicing these exercises A must have realized that although he is allowing B to hold him, he can with one thought and move, change the whole situation. In other words he can be the one to hold B. Thinking in this way is a positive way of thinking a "plus" way of life. It means that A does not need to depend on B to set him free.

Do not let a person excuse himself by saying, "I'm not to blame, because I'm bad and had no choice.", or "I've turned out bad because my parents are bad." Simply waiting for things to improve by themselves will result in nothing. If a person depends solely on changes in the environment, he will suffer greatly; for to wait for society to improve without doing anything for oneself is like waiting for polluted waters to become pure by themselves. Although the social environment may remain the same, it should be possible to change ourselves. We must realize that as far as ourselves go, changing the negative into the positive may depend only upon one well-timed turn in the direction of the spirit and one change of method.

If a person has understood this, he will be all right no matter how his environment may change.

[10]

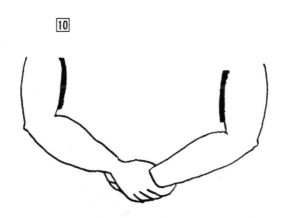

35. KATATETORI RYOTEMOCHI KOKYUNAGE (1)

Standing in right hanmi, B hold A's left hand in both hands. (photo 234) Since B keeps one point, A will not be able to move his left hand. A, in left hanmi, relaxes his right arm and maintains a steady, outward flow of Ki. A moves in directly toward B. As A does so, A's strength and B's will move in the same direction (photo 235).

236

Without altering the position of his right arm, A swings his hips to the right and steps both with his right foot to B's rear and brings his left foot to his right (photo 236). A's left arm and B's Ki is directed through the fingers of A's left hand. Now A can lead B freely with his left hand.

235

234

237

238

A brings down his left arm (photo 237) and then brings it up in a circle as he did in UDEMAWASHI UNDO (photo 238). B's body will follow. Then A points the fingertips of his left hand toward B's face and B will fall backward (photo 239). Next A can do the whole movement in one motion. As A approaches B, A must pour a powerful stream of Ki from his eyes and look straight into B's face. B will reply unconsciously by shooting Ki from his eyes to combat A's. One moment before the two Ki collide, A turns his face in the same direction as B as he turns his whole body to the right, letting B follow his own inertia, which, as A brings down his arm in a circle, will lead B into a fall. This process is called evoking B's Ki.

Next A can lead B at the moment B comes to grip A's hand.

239

Fifth Level

36. ZAGI HANDACHI SHOMENUCHI KOKYUNAGE

A sits on his knees facing B. B stands and tries to strike A's forehead with his right hand (photo 240).

When B's Ki starts, A swings up his right hand in IKKYO UNDO to the outside of B's right arm. B's Ki will be deflected along A's arm and to the ground (photo 241).

240

241

242

243

As he deflects B's arm, A turns his body to the right and brings down B's arm with his right hand and B's neck with his left (photo 242).

In the standing position, A can continue turning his body but in the sitting position A cannot move his body so much.

When A is sitting, B must lower his body to strike A. A must bring down B's neck as if to move B's face down to the ground. After B's neck is lowered, he will come up as a reaction. A helps B's movement upward by swinging up his hand. B will be led upward and fall down (photo 243).

37. ZAGI HANDACHI MUNETSUKI KOTEGAESHI

A sits facing B. B tries to strike A's chest with his right fist (photo 244). At the moment B's fist touches A's chest, A turns his body to the right on his left knee. B's fist passes by A. A brings down B's fist with his left hand. B will fall forward (photo 245).

A leads B's fist upward, turns his wrist (photo 246), and bring it down with the help of his right hand. B will fall down (photo 247). A instantly slides his right hand down along B's right arm to the elbow and turns B's body with both hands to make B lie face down (photo 248).

245

244

A pins B down in the same manner as MUNETSUKI KOTE-
GAESHI in the standing position (photo 249).

38. ZAGI HANDACHI YOKOMENUCHI KOKYUNAGE

A sits facing B. B swings up his right open hand and tries to strike the left side of A's face (photo 250).

A turns his body to the left on his right knee, kneeling with his toes bent forward, and swings up both arms in a relaxed manner (photo 251).

As B loses his balance and falls forward, A strikes his right arm with his left hand and his neck with his right hand.

B will fall in a somersault (photo 252).

A should not really hit B's arm and neck, but instead extends Ki well with both hands and hits B with Ki. B will fall down before A's hands touch his body.

250

251

252

253 254

39. MUNETSUKI KOKYUNAGE (ZEMPONAGE)

A stands in right hanmi. B takes a step with his right foot and strikes A's chest with his right fist (photo 253).

A turns his body to the right as he takes a step backward on his right foot. B's fist will miss A's body (photo 254).

A leads B's fist in his right hand and B's elbow in his left first down lightly and immediately, using B's reaction, upward to lead B's Ki upward (photo 255). When B's body comes down in the reaction, A brings down B's arm and B will fall (photo 256, 257).

When A takes a step backward, his right foot and left foot should be in a line parallel to the line of B's attack. Then A can lead B forward without colliding against B's force.

Now let's review the Five Principles of Shin-Shin Toitsu Aikido.

1. Extending Ki

When B comes to strike A, A must extend Ki strongly. Otherwise B's strong Ki will penetrate.

2. Know your opponent's mind

A understands very well that B is coming to strike him.

3. Respect your opponent's Ki

A must lead B in the same direction as B's attack. If A turns his body too much to the right, he is obliged to change B's direction, which will collid against B's force.

255

256

4.　　Put yourself in your opponent's place

A must put his body in a position so that he can hold B's right arm in a relaxed way.

5.　　Perform with confidence.

A leads B with the up and down movements of his one point.

The Five Principles are applicable not only to Aikido techniques but also to daily life. In practising the techniques of Shin-Shin Toitsu Aikido, one must learn them with both his mind and body. Then one will be able to live without colliding against others.

257

40. MUNETSUKI KOKYU NAGE (SUDORI)

A stands in right hanmi. B takes a step his right foot and strikes A's chest with his right fist (photo 258).

If A keeps one point, he can feel B's Ki come before his fist moves. When B's Ki starts, A takes a step on his left foot forward and drops to his right knee. A must make his body as low and rounded as possible and steady himself by putting his hands on the floor (photo 259).

B finds only empty air where he thinks A's body should be, but he is nevertheless unable to stop his action. Feeling the contact of A's body on his lower legs, he will topple over A and down (photo 260).

When B moves in for the strike, A should not give his plan away by looking down. Instead, A should lead B's Ki astray by looking up toward B.

258

259

260

41. MUNETSUKI KOKYU NAGE (KAITEN NAGE)

A stands in right hanmi. B takes a step on his right foot and attempts to strike A's chest with his right fist (photo 261).

A takes a step backward on his right foot and lets B strike empty air. At the same time A presses down on B's right wrist with his left hand, and then puts his right hand lightly on B's lowered head (photo 262).

Holding B's right hand with his left hand, A guides it up behind B's right side (photo 263). Then with his right hand which is still on B's lowered neck, he pushes B in the direction of his movement.

B will roll over once and fall in that direction (photo 264).

After A has mastered the form of this technique, let him practise throwing B in one fluid move. He should throw B while retreating a little when B attacks.

261

262

263

264

265   266

42. KATATETORI RYOTEMOCHI KOTEGAESHI

A stands in left hanmi and thrusts his left hand forward. B, in a right hanmi, holds A's left hand as if holding a sword with both hands. In this case B keeps one point and extends Ki through his arms up to A's left shoulder (photo 265).

A puts himself in B's place in the same way as KATATETORI RYOTEMOCHI KOKYUNAGE (P 140, 141) and then swings up both arms (photo 266, 267, 268).

B will lose his balance forward when A swings down both arms. A holds B's left wrist in a KOTEGAESHI hold with his right hand (photo 269).

A continues the circular movement to lead B's left wrist up and turns his wrist (photo 270) and helps to bring down B's wrist with his left hand. B will fall (photo 271).

A pins B in the same manner as the other KOTEGAESHI throws.

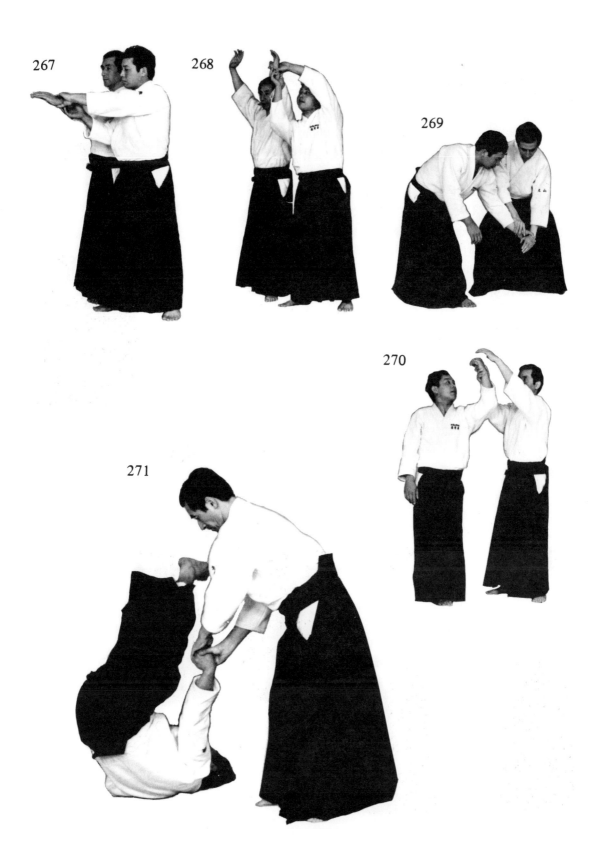

43 KATATETORI RYOTEMOCHI
KOKYUNAGE (2)

A stands in left hanmi and B stands in right hanmi and holds A's left hand with both hands (photo 272).

A puts himself in B's place in the same manner as KATATETOR RYOTEMOCHI KOKYUNAGE (I) and brings down his left hand and swings his right hand to the rear when he draws his left foot to the right (photo 275).

Before B's body settles down, A jumps behind B and throws B in the same manner as KATATE-KOSATORI KOKYUNAGE (photo 276~279).

274

273

272

275

276

277

278

279

280

281

44. YOKOMENUCHI KOTEGAESHI

A stands in left hanmi. B swings up his right hand, takes a step with his right foot, and attempts to strike the left side of A's face. (photo 280).

A takes a step forward with his right foot and pivots to the right and steps backward with his left foot as he swings his arms up and down to lead down B's right arm (photo 281).

A continues the movement by swinging up B's right wrist with his left hand (phto 282). A turns B's right wrist in a KOTEGAESHI way and helps to bring it down with his left hand. B will fall (photo 283).

282

283

45. YOKOMENUCHI KOKYU NAGE (2)

A stands in left hanmi. B swings up his right hand and steps with his right foot to strike the left side of A's face (photo 284).

A swings up both hands as he takes a large step backward with his left foot. He then leads down B's right hand and holds it with his right hand from above. He then draws his right foot to the left and swings his left hand to the rear (photo 285). Since A has swung his hips to the left, his weight will naturally be on his left foot. Using the reflex motion, A leaps to B's right rear as he swings up B's right hand (photo 286). At the same time as his feet land the ground, A wraps his left hand around B's neck and leads B's body down together with his right hand. His right hand throws B's hand down (photo 287). A then swings up his right hand to lead B upward (photo 288). A throws B as in SHOMENUCHI KOKYUNAGE (p.92 . 93.) (photo 289).

286

287

288

289

290

291

46. SHOMENUCHI KOTEGAESHI

This technique begins the same as SHOMEN-
UCHI KOKYUNAGE, except that, instead of putting his left hand on B's neck, A takes B's right
wrist in his left hand.

A helps B's downward strike with his left hand
so that B falls forward (photo 291). Using B's
reaction, A leads B upward (photo 292).

A turns B's wrist in KOTEGAESHI and brings it
down with the help of his right hand and throws B
(photo 293).

292

293

294

295

47. SHOMENUCHI IKKYO

IRIMI

A stands in right hanmi and B tries to strike A's forehead with his right hand (photo 294). A swings up his arms so that his right hand touches B's right wrist and his left hand touches B's right elbow (photo 295). As soon as A touches B's arm, he moves B's arm in an arch back towards B and straight down (photo 296). As A continues his movement by taking a large step forward with his left foot, B will fall on his stomach (photo 297). A then kneels on his toes, left knee in B's armpit and pins B's arm. B's pinned arm should be a little higher than his shoulder. If A pushes B's arm down, B will be able to stand up. A must keep one point and lightly touch B's arm. Then B will be unable to stand up. A should also stretch B's arm a bit, from B's wrist, then B's Ki will stop at his arm. This makes it more difficult for B to stand up.

When A changes the direction of B's arm (photo 295), A should not push it back as in figure a. A must keep one point and relax his arms and swing them up as in IKKYO UNDO to lead B's power down as in figure b.

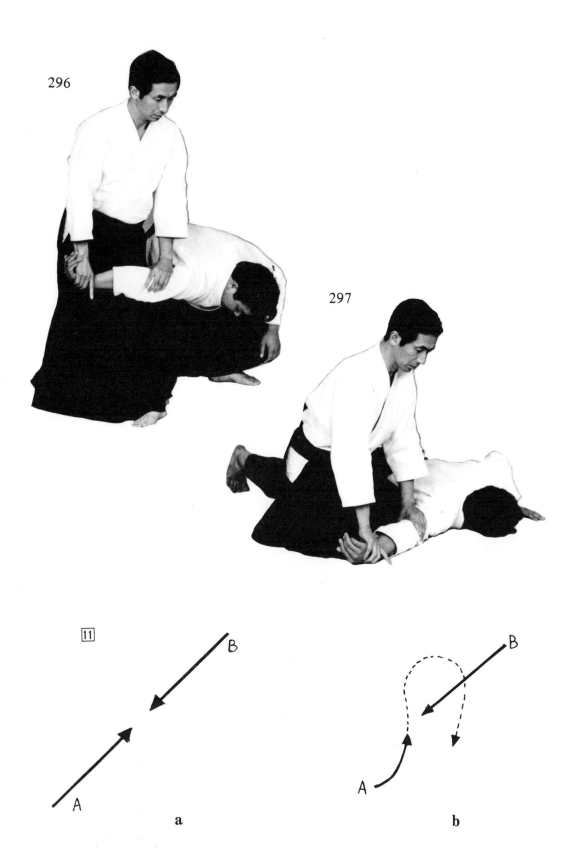

296

297

11

A

B

a

A

B

b

165

TENKAN

When B begins to strike, A steps foward with his left foot, and to the rear of B, while swinging up his arms (photo 299). A then swings B's arm down towards the ground as he turns to the right (photo 300). B will move around A and fall (photo 301).

A should not pull B's arm to the side. B will resist. A must simply bring B's arm downward, using weight underside and B will naturally follow.

298

299

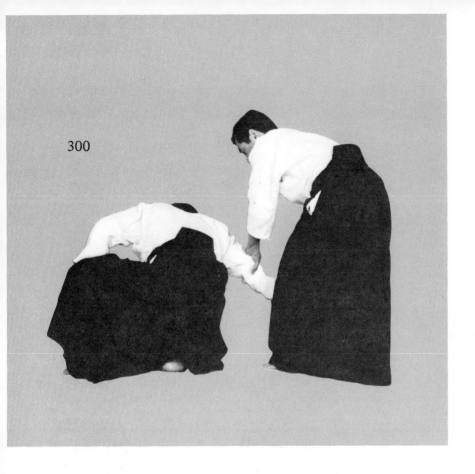

300

301

302

303

304

48. USHIRO TEKUBITORI KOTEGAESHI

B stands behind A and holds A's wrists (photo 302). A leads B's hands upward as in USHIRO TEKUBITORI KOKYUNAGE (p.122). As he does so A takes a short step backwards with his left foot without moving the upper body (photo 303). A then takes a deep step back on his right foot and leads B down by bending his upper body forward (photo 304). When B loses his balance, A seizes B's right wrist with his left hand in a KOTEGAESHI hold (photo 305) and applies KOTEGAESHI to throw B (photo 306, 307).

305

306

307

169

308   309   310

49. USHIRO TEKUBITORI IKKYO

B stands behind A and holds his wrists (photo 308). A bends both wrists and points his fingers upward and leads B's hands up as A steps back on his left foot (photo 309). He then takes a deep step back on his right foot and bends his upper body to lead B forward and down (photo 311). A puts his right hand on B's elbow (photo 312), takes B's wrist with his left hand, and bends B's wrist so his fingers are pointing forward (photo 313). A straightens up his body and leads B down (photo 314).

When A straightens up his body, he should not move B's arm. A should extend Ki through B's elbow, then straighten up. B's wrist will naturally come up and consequently B will fall since his elbow will act as a lever on his body.

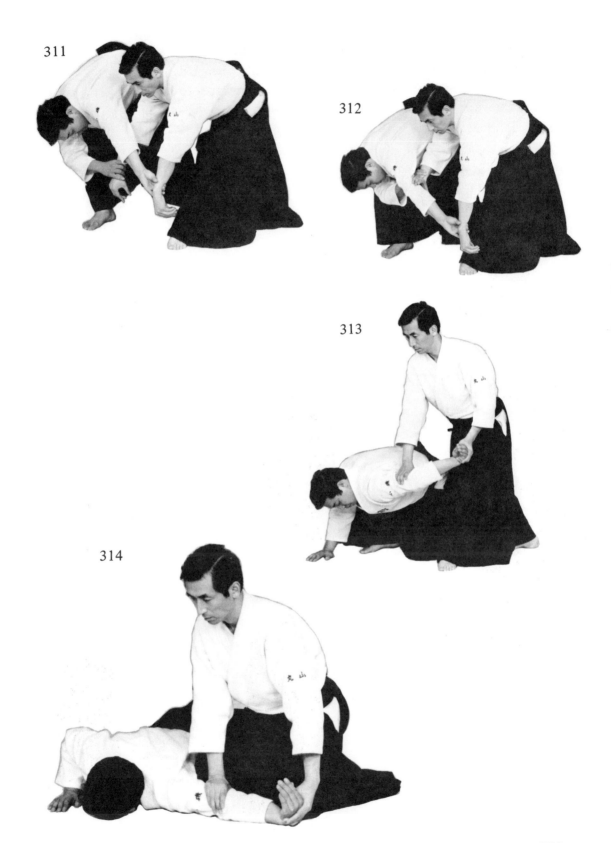

I have explained USHIROTEKUBITORI techniques from a static position. Now I will explain them when B is moving to attack A.

A stands in right hanmi and holds out his right hand (photo 315). B rushes towards A, grabbing A's right wrist with his right·hand. B continues around to the back of A and grabs A's left wrist. B then puts his knee at the base of A's spine and pulls A's wrists to the rear. This will cause A to collapse.

315

316

317

318

When B tries to grab A's right hand, A leads B's right hand down and keeps his Ki extending towards B. When B tries to leap behind A, A's leading B will cause him to run around A (photo 316). A then bends his right wrist to turn the fingers upward and lowers his whole body causing B to lose his balance (photo 317). A stands up and brings his right hand towards B's face (photo 318), and then leads B's arm down with the help of his left hand on B's elbow (photo 319).

319

320

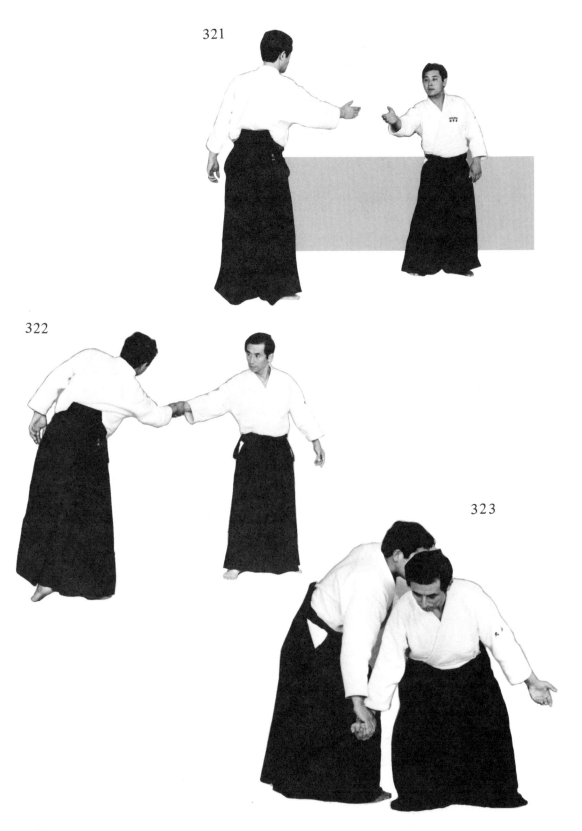

321

322

323

174

When A leads B down and behind him, he offers B his left hand to get B to continue around him. As B continues around, A raises both hands and B will then take A's left hand (photo 324). When A feels B's power on his wrists when he raises them, A takes a step forward on his left foot and swings down both his hands. B will be thrown forward (photo 325). This is USHIRO TEKUBITORI KOKYU-NAGE

325

324

SIXTH LEVEL

TANTO TORI

It would be of no use practising techniques in the training hall if one became upset when facing a real situation. One must be able to keep calm in every situation. That's why we have been practising to keep one point and extend Ki. As I have always explained, if one is calm and has mind and body unified, there is a great amount of power available to him.

Now let's practise TANTO-TORI (knife attacks). We use a wooden knife (TANTO). However we must always consider it to be a real knife. By practising with a wooden knife which we consider to be real we can learn to keep calm if when attacked with a real knife.

This also holds true in daily activities. One must deal with all daily activities, large and small, with Ki extended.

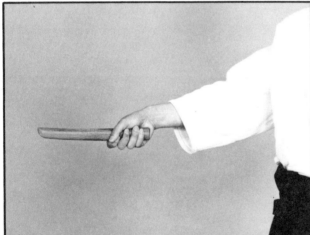

326

327

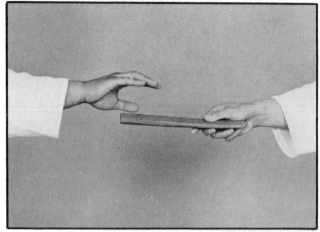

328

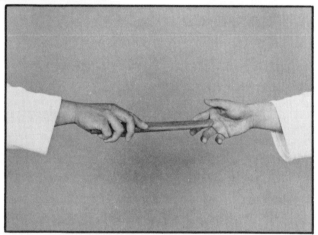

329

We should not touch the blade of the TANTO during practice, as we consider it to be a real knife. Before explaining the techniques, I will explain how to hold a TANTO. One holds the TANTO either with the blade down (photo 326), or blade up (photo 327). In most TANTO TORI techniques we hold it with the blade down (photo 326), except when mentioned otherwise.

How to hand a TANTO to your partner.

After A takes the TANTO away from B, A returns it to B in the following manner: A holds the TANTO in his right hand taking care not to touch the blade, as in photo 328, and offers the handle to B. A should also be extending Ki through the TANTO. As B takes the handle, as in photo 329, he can immediately attack A. So A must move into the proper MA–AI as soon as B takes the TANTO. When one gives a knife, one should not offer the blade to the other person. One must always offer the handle so that the other person can hold it easily without danger.

330

331

50. SHOMENUCHI KOKYUNAGE

A stands in right hanmi. B holds a TANTO with his right hand and tries to strike A's forehead (photo 330). A swings up his right hand, as in IKKYO UNDO, extending Ki along the outside of B's right arm. The TANTO will be deflected and continue towards the ground (phto 331). A then takes a step forward with his left foot and turns to the right facing B. A brings his right hand down on B's right upperarm and his left hand down on B's neck (photo 332). Making use of B's reaction to stand up, A swings his right hand up towards B's face to lead B's Ki upward (photo 333). When A extends Ki toward B's face with his right hand, B will fall. To control B's right arm, A lets it slide through his right hand so that when B is completely on the ground, A is holding B's right wrist between his right hand and right thigh(photo 334).

332

333

178

334

335

336

A then takes B's right hand with his left hand and slides his right hand up along B's right arm with his fingers bent. A's bent fingers will naturally touch the handle of the TANTO (photo 335). A walks around B's head to turn B's body over and take away the TANTO (photo 336).

In the position of photo 333, to keep B from cutting A as B falls, A must keep B's head close to his right shoulder with his left hand. As long as B's head is kept next to A's shoulder, B's right arm is unable to cut him. A must lead B straight down from that position and immediately hold B's right arm so that B has no time to attack him.

337   338

51. MUNETSUKI KOTEGAESHI

A stands in left hanmi. B holds a TANTO in his right hand and tries to thrust at A's chest (photo 337). A moves in the same way as MUNETSUKI KOTEGAESHI without a weapon, leading B's right hand around him and down (photo 338, 339). Following the rhythm of B's reaction, A applies KOTEGAESHI to B's hand (photo 340) and throws B as he takes the TANTO away (photo 341). Then A swings the TANTO to the rear to prepare for an attack from behind.

To take away the TANTO, A puts the base of his index finger on the top of the handle and pushes it down in the direction of B's fingers (photo 342, 343).

339   340

180

341

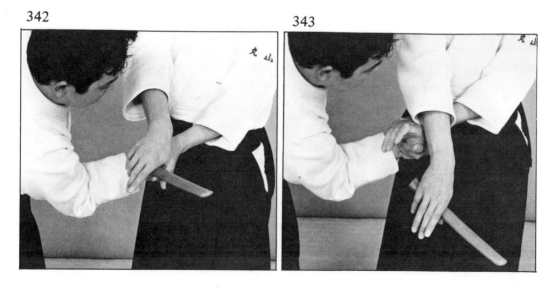

342   343

52. YOKOMENUCHI SHIHONAGE

A stands in left hanmi. B holds the TANTO in his right hand and tries to cut, from the left side of A's neck down to A's right side while advancing with his right foot (photo 344). A moves into B by taking a step forward on his right foot, with his left hand protecting his face (photo 345). A continues this movement by pivoting to the left on his right foot and taking a step back on his left foot, then drawing his right foot to his left foot. A's left hand leads B's hand down and into both A's hands (photo 346). A continues this movement to execute SHIHONAGE IRIMI and takes away the TANTO as he throws B. In YOKOMENUCHI SHIHONAGE without TANTO, A steps back when attacked. But when B attacks with a TANTO or sword, A will be cut if he steps back. A must move into B, parallel with B's line of attack, and bring his left hand up to protect his face (figure 12).

When A takes away the TANTO, if he uses his left hand, he risks cutting his fingers if his left hand slips. It is better to use the right hand sliding it down so that his thumb pushes the end of the handle and the little finger holds the top of the TANTO (photo 350, 351).

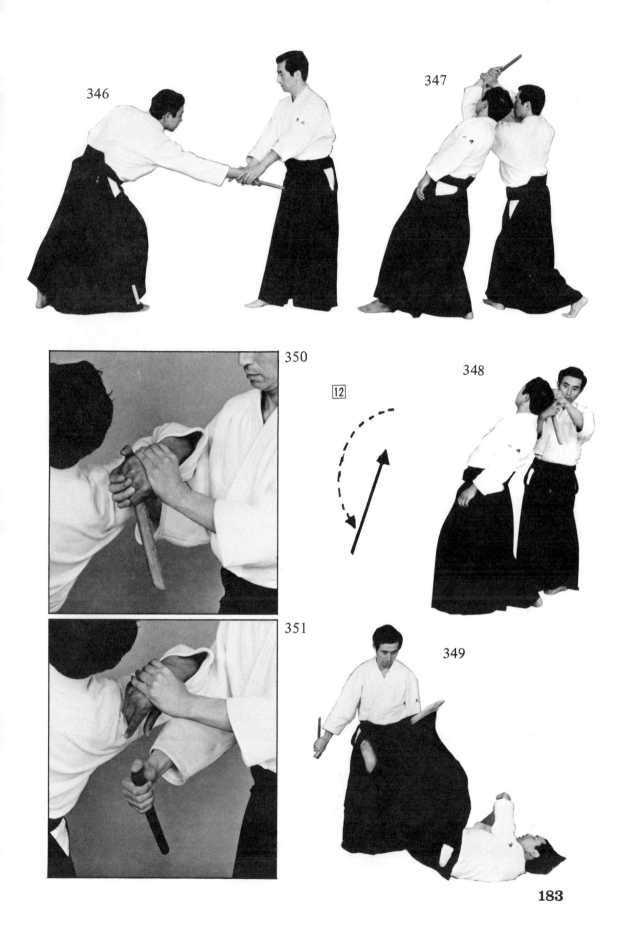

346

347

350

348

12

349

351

53. YOKOMENUCHI GOKYO

A stands in left hanmi. B holds the TANTO in his right hand with "BLADE UP" and tries to stab A in the face (photo 352). At the moment B swings up the TANTO, A steps forward with his left foot, keeping left hanmi, as he swings up his hand. A's left hand pushes up B's right forearm and his right hand comes at the left side of B's chest. B's right hand is extended backwards and his body leans backwards, too (photo 353). A continues to block B's right arm with his left hand and takes B's right wrist with his right hand. A's right arm is unbendable so B cannot cut A with the TANTO. If A holds B's right wrist like in IKKYO, A will be cut by B (photo 354, 359). A keeps B's right wrist in his right hand and moves under B's arm and takes B's right elbow in his left hand (photo 355). Then A swings down B's arm (photo 356), and B turns around A and falls on his stomach (photo 357). A pushes B's right wrist toward his shoulder with his right hand and at the same time pulls B's right elbow up with his left hand.

354

352

353

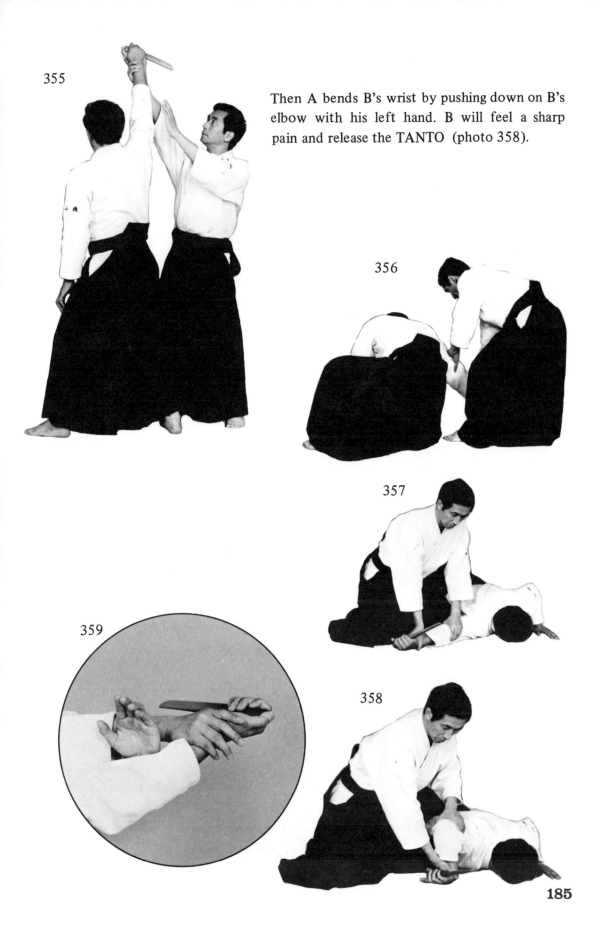

355

Then A bends B's wrist by pushing down on B's elbow with his left hand. B will feel a sharp pain and release the TANTO (photo 358).

356

357

359

358

185

A must practise well how to jump in as he swings up both hands. First A must practise IKKYO UNDO. Next he turns his body sideways with his left shoulder leading and swings his hands up without moving his shoulders (photo 360). His left hand swings up to eyelevel and his right hand to the left side of his chest. When A swings up his hands, B tries to bend A's arms. They should be unbendable. Next B pushes up on A's right hand. If A is keeping one point, the weight of his right hand is underside and will not move. B stands in front of A and pushes back A's hands. If A is extending Ki, he is immovable. A must repeat this exercise so that he can jump in quickly when B swings up the TANTO.

After A jumps in, if he simply extends Ki downward, B will fall. This is YOKOMENUCHI KOKYUNAGE IRIMI.

360

The founder initiates the author into the deepest understandings of swords.

(3)

361

362

363

54. USHIROTSUKI KOTEGAESHI

A stands naturally while B stands behind him with a TANTO in his right hand pointed at A's back. A first raises his hands (photo 361).

Remember that since B threatens to stab A if A moves, A should remain still until he can throw and disarm B in one single moment.

A keeps one point and in a single move pivots to the right on his right foot, and lowers his right hand to lead B's right hand forward (photo 362). A then takes B's right wrist in his left hand, and throws and disarms B as he does in KOTEGAESHI (photo 364, 365, 366).

364

365

366

55. YONINGAKE (Four Men Attack)

So far I have been explaining techniques against one attacker. As explained in HAPPO UNDO, one must extend Ki in the direction one is facing. When one extends Ki to the thing one is doing at that moment, one is doing one's best.

It is easy to deal with one difficulty at a time. However many people give up when faced with many difficulties. Whatever happens, one must extend Ki to each situation. We practise the four men attack in Shin-Shin Toitsu Aikido in order to practise this.

A stands naturally while four people stand around A keeping MA-AI. Then the four people attack A simultaneously. A must deal with each attacker keeping unification of mind and body. As long as A is moving, A faces only one attacker at a time. A must remember that to do YONINGAKE, he must practise each technique in detail.

CONCLUSION

CONCLUSION

I hope to contribute to the education of the younger generation through this book. The application of Shin-Shin Toitsu Aikido is infinite. The basis being the Four Basic Principles to Unify Mind and Body, which are the principles of the universe. They are the principles which everyone must agree with and cannot deny. That is why we can call it a Way of Life.

What is lacking in modern education is the extension of Ki. As long as one is extending Ki, one never receives the Ki of others and can never be beaten. Ki flows naturally to others. Violent students are those who have lost all hope in society. They are too weak. Today's teachers should try to become strong and to extend positive Ki. In this way the students will also extend positive Ki. It is my hope that all teachers will learn how to extend Ki through the practice of Shin-Shin Toitsu Aikido and provide a good example for the next generation. I also hope that the younger generation learns to extend Ki and to control themselves, independent from the changes of society.

In Shin-Shin Toitsu Aikido, we give the examinations of Ki before those of Aikido. There are three beginning levels, Shokyu, Chukyu, and Jokyu. One must be Jokyu level to take the examination of first dan in Aikido. It is because Aikido is impossible without the unification of mind and body.

I tried to explain thoroughly the Four Basic Principles to Unify Mind and Body. However it is difficult to learn about the workings of the mind from books. It would be better to learn from qualified instructors.

I have a dream of spreading Shin-Shin Toitsu Aikido to every country in the world. I also hope that those who have practised Aikido without knowing about the unification of mind and body will come to understand Shin-Shin Toitsu Aikido.

In this way if everyone extends positive Ki, and lives a bright and happy life, then peace in this world and a bright future for all is not impossible.

APPENDIX

APPENDIX

1. About the Hakama

The hakama worn with the white dogi used to be the formal wear of Aikido practitioners. But this has been changed with the process of time. Today only those who have attained a high level of proficiency are allowed to wear the hakama. For beginners footwork is very important, if they wore the hakama, it would be difficult to correct their footwork. The hakama is also a goal for beginners to work towards. However many women have special permission to put them on since they prefer to look elegant.

A. The use of the hakama

(a). One point is more easily maintained.

The first use of wearing the hakama is that it helps the wearer to keep one point. With only a dogi and a belt on, the belt tends to move up and down whenever it is pulled. This may have the effect of moving the person's feelings, which should be settled at the one point, up and down accordingly. In contrast to this the proper way of wearing the hakama over the belt presses the knot of the belt against the lower abdomen so that it is fixed at the one point and will not move. This gives a feeling of greater stability to the wearer. Upon gaining the right to wear hakamas, people tend to make quick progress in the art. This is partly due to their self-confidence in having earned that right, but also in large part to their one point having become set as a result of wearing the hakama.

(b) The whole uniform is kept orderly.

Students are often seen fastening the belt in the middle of a Judo match. But in an actual situation there is no time to do that. Wearing the hakama will prevent the uniform from getting loose no matter how wildly the wearer may move. But before wearing the hakama, it is necessary to learn how to put it on correctly. No one whose hakama comes loose during practice should have the right to wear one, for it indicates he has not even learned to put it on correctly.

(c) The hakama makes for stability.

Besides helping to maintain the one point, the hakama adds to the feeling of stability by giving the wearer an appearance of solidity since his body forms a tetrahedron triangle with it on. In stark contrast to this, wearing a big jacket and tight trousers gives one the form of an inverted triangle. This form gives no impression of stability whatsoever. While it is true that the mind moves the body, the mind itself may be influenced by outward circumstances. Thus in turn the stability of the mind, which is influenced by outward forms, influences the stability of our body without our knowing it.

(d). The hakama makes for calmness.

When a person lectures in a large hall, a cloth is usually draped over the table in front of him to hide his feet from the audience. One, who is inexperienced at giving lectures, may sometimes lose his calm only because the audience can see his legs beneath the table. Similarly wearing the hakama also hides the feet of the person who has just attained a high rank and helps him keep calm. Moreover, people looking on will not be able to tell if his steps get a little bit out of order.

In this section some points on the meaning of the hakama have been given. But remember also that in Aikido calmness must always be retained as a matter of course whether a hakama is worn or not. There is no denying that the hakama does make a great difference in the beginning. But one must not become dependent on it and must rise above its influence. This is the message of the saying, "A great man is never moved by circumstances." On the other hand, there is another saying which complements the preceding one, "True though that may be, circumstances also form the spirit." Thus in pursuit of the genuine calmness that is untouched by any calamity, a person uses circumstances to help him develop a serene spirit. In this sense there is meaning in endeavoring to keep one point through the use of the hakama.

(e) How to fasten the belt.

Figure 1. First grasp the middle of the belt with your right hand and place it against your one point.

Figure 2. Keeping it there, take the ends of the belt around to the back. Then crossing the ends at the back, bring them to the front. Then tie the knot of the belt right at the one point, tying the belt neither too loosely nor too tightly. If it is too loose, the uniform will soon become disarranged. If it is tied too tightly, it may cause an uncomfortable feeling of pressure which will be a distraction and hinder the spirit from calming itself at the one point. You must first keep one point and then adjust the tightness of the belt accordingly.

Figure 3. Cross the belt in the right hand over with the belt in the left hand at the one point. Then pass the end that goes over the other beneath all the belt already wound around the body. Tie that end into a knot with the other end of the belt. In this last step, one end of the belt gathers up the whole belt before being tied into a knot with the other. This prevents the belt from getting loose.

(f). How to put the hakama on.

Figure 1. Stepping into the hakama, place the front of the hakama, (the front is the side without the backing), on the upper part of the belt and take the loose ends of the front straps to the back.

Figure 2. Crossing the ends of the straps in back, bring them to the front again.

Figure 3. Tie a small knot with them just below the covered belt knot so that the front top of the

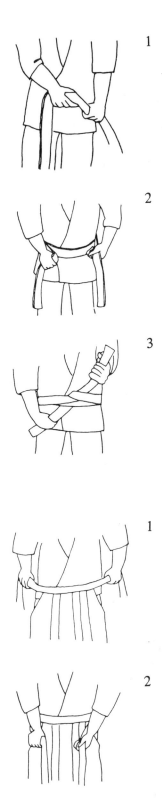

1

2

3

1

2

hakama above it and this knot below it, will keep the belt knot in place.

Figure 4. Cross the remaining ends of the front straps at the back and wind the rest around the hips. As much as possible it is better not to tie a knot behind the hips because the knot may hurt the hip muscles if it is forced against them in the course of taking a fall. If a knot has to be tied at the back, make it as small as possible.

Figure 5. Put the back support of the hakama on top of the belt in the back.

Figure 6. At both sides of the hips, bring down the back straps as shown in the sketch. Be sure to go under both the front straps of the hakama and the belt, then pull the back straps down firmly. This will prevent the back support from getting loose and falling down. Bring both back straps to the front and tie them in a knot. When tying them in the front, do it so that the knot catches on the first hakama knot.

The hakama must also be tied neither too loosely nor too tightly. Since the front and back straps of the hamaka hold the belt between them, the belt will not move even if the dogi is pulled.

(g) How to fold the hakama

Leaving the hakama carelessly about after using it will wrinkle it. Folding it neatly after usage will keep the pleats sharp without having to iron them. It will also make for a neat and sharp appearance the next time it is worn. So to acquire this good habit, always fold the hakama neatly.

Figure 1. First place the hakama on the floor with its front face down. Arrange the back and front straps, one on top of the other. Straighten the pleats down the center of the back carefully following the folding creases. Then straighten out the sides of the hakama from the back support to the hem.

Figure 2. Flip the back support over with the left hand. Then holding the support and the top

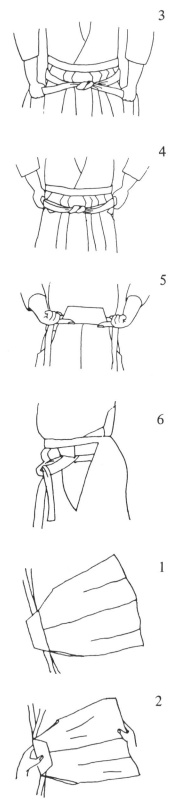

front of the hakama with the left hand and the hems of the front and back with the right hand, stretch the hakama tightly.

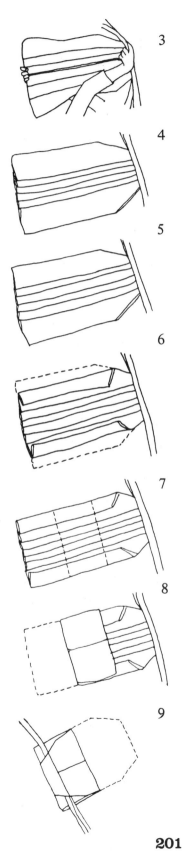

3

Figure 3. Turn the hakama over with both hands in one move. This time the back of the hakama should face down. In turning the hakama over, be sure to keep the hakama stretched tightly to prevent the pleats down the center of the back from being disarranged.

However in turning the hakama over, it does not matter if the other parts are disturbed. Now arrange the front of the hakama.

4

Figure 4. Carefully lay the front and back hakama straps on top of each other. Stretch out, smooth, and align the folds along the slanting side openings of both the front and the back. In doing this do not disturb the part already ordered in the back, and arrange both the front and back so that their hems are well stretched and their side openings lie neatly on top of each other.

5

Figure 5. Working from the outside in, arrange each pleat in accordance with the correct crease marks. Again in doing this, do not move the back part of the hakama which you have already arranged.

6

Figure 6. Fold both outer edges of the hakama inward so that nothing is left farther out than the top of the hakama.

7

Figure 7. Lightly pat along the lines marked by the dotted lines in the sketch. This will make it easier to fold the hakama into three parts.

Figure 8. Fold the hakama from the hem at the first dotted line.

8

Figure 9. Now fold the upper part of the hakama over to the left, and straighten the back support which was hidden under the front side.

The following explanation will teach you how to fold the straps.

9

Figure 1. Turn the back support of the hakama so it faces you. Pull the short straps attached to the back of the hakama towards you, and the long straps attached to the front, lay to the side of the hakama.

Figure 2. After straightening out any wrinkles or twists in the long straps of the right side, fold it in half twice. Then put it on the hakama slanting the strap diagonally across to the left.

Figure 3. Arrange the long left strap in the same way. But slant it to the right so that it will cross the straps from the right side.

Figure 4. Pass the short, right strap over and under the crossing of the two long straps, and bring it straight towards you.

Figure 5. Secure the place where the short strap crosses over the long ones by passing the short strap to the right, over itself and under the long strap. Then pull the free end toward you.

Figure 6. Pull the end of the short strap further towards you to get rid of all the slack. Then fold it upward to the left, in the direction it naturally tends to fold and place it on the long strap.

Figure 7. In the same way, pass the short strap of the left side through the center, crossing of the two long straps. Then pass the free end of the crossing of the two long straps. Then pass the free end of the short strap over and under itself and the left long strap. Finally stretch this short strap up to the right. In stretching it upward, pass it under the short strap on the right side. This will make each band secure since they are held down in turn by another band as shown in Figure 7.

After being folded in this way, the creases of the hakama will remain in their correct place; and, the hakama will retain its proper shape, no matter how small the hakama may be folded for carrying about.

Many people forget the proper way of fixing

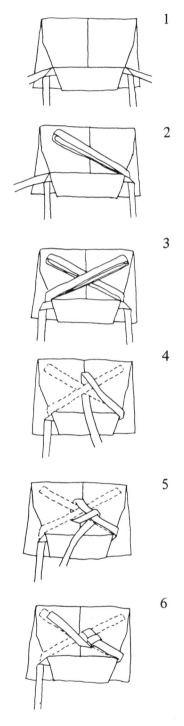

the straps. They can learn and remember the method easier by remembering the   following directions:

1. Pass through the center of the universe. (Figure 4)
2. Govern the self. (Figure 5)
3. Walk the right way. (Figure 6)

This should be easy to remember because they are Aikido principles.

The noble spirit is certain to find expression in one's appearance. If a man's spirit is integrated and ordered, naturally his behavior and actions are integrated and ordered too. Likewise his appearance is integrated and ordered; his shirt is kept under his belt, and his tie is straight and neat.

Some people think that appearance does not count as long as the spirit is upright. In meals, indeed, what matters is the food and not the inedible tableware. Yet it is human and understandable to desire the better tableware for the more delicious food. No matter how delicious the food, it would lose its flavor if served on a dirty plate. These views do not advocate extravagant clothing or a gourmet's taste. But they do advise parents to help their child to develop during his childhood not only by emphasizing an upright spirit but also the habit of keeping his appearance tidy and of always being clean.

B. About Footwear

Upon entering a training hall, students should always put their footwear where they are told to do so. If there is nowhere for them to be put away, the students should arrange them as in the sketch after taking them off. Then they can easily and quickly put them on when leaving the hall. This is proper etiquette.

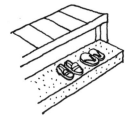

In olden days the Japanese samurai considered it shameful to rush out in an emergency barefoot and in great confusion. When one takes off his footwear, there is time to arrange them properly for quick use. For the samurai to be able to wear them immediately meant having his spirit prepared against any emergency. Therefore it was an important habit. If the spirit is always prepared, there is no need for frantic confusion no matter what the emergency may be.

Do not carelessly scorn the idea of arranging footwear as something trivial. To be alert and pay full attention even to tiny things is to train the spirit. Particularly being attentive to footwear is like watching one's steps. Calming the spirit by settling oneself at the one point also implies that one is watching one's steps. On the other hand becoming agitated means that the eyes no longer turn towards one's steps and one will begin to stumble against objects and problems and fall over.

The following story is from a training hall in Higashikurume in Tokyo. A student's parents came to watch their seven year old son practise Shin-Shin Toitsu Aikido.

Entering the hall, they saw about 20 slippers and shoes arranged in one neat row. The father asked me, "Does someone arrange these?" I answered, "No, each child arranges his own when he takes them off." The couple turned to each other and began discussing something. Then the father came over and said, "Well, now I know! You see recently I began noticing that the slippers and shoes in our home were always put away in their proper places. Even the slippers in the toilet are arranged in order. I thought all the time that my wife was doing it, but just now I realized I was wrong. It must have been our seven year old son! He did not tell us anything."

Since then the students parents have been telling all their friends about this. Thanks to them many children have enrolled.

GLOSSARY OF AIKIDO TERMS

CHOYAKU UNDO: the exercise where one leaps as he executes a movement

FUNEKOGI: a rowing motion

HANMI: A posture with one foot advanced, and the body weight equally distributed on both feet.

HAPPO: eight directions.

IKKYO: the most basic of the Aikido ways to control an opponent's arm.

IRIMI: the non-colliding method of leading an opponent's Ki so that the technique can be applied by moving inside the opponent's direct line of attack. (Compare with tenkan.)

IRIMI-ATE: irimi thrust.

KAITEN-NAGE: the spin throw which makes the opponent's body revolve once before he is led down.

KANSETSU-WAZA: techniques which are applied to the joints.

KATA-TORI: an opponent's attack by seizing one's shoulder.

KATATE-TORI: an opponent's attack by seizing one's arm.

KOHO-TENTO falling backward.

KOKYU-NAGE: The throw which overthrows the opponent using his own momentum and the timing of one's mind and body, but without applying any pressure to his joints.

KOTE-GAESHI: the wrist twist.

KUBI-SHIME: an opponent's strangle hold.

MA-AI: the correct distance or interval between two opposing parties.

MUNE-TSUKI: an opponent's attack by striking one's chest.

RYOKATA-TORI: an opponent's attack by gripping both of one's shoulders

SAYU: term indicating left and right directions.

SEIZA: sitting on one's knees with the back straight.

SHIHO-NAGE: One of the basic Aikido throws.

SHOMEN-UCHI: an opponent's attack by striking directly down on one's head.

TEKUBI-KOSA: crossed wrists.

TENKAN: method of turning outside of the opponent's line of attack, while simultaneously leading his Ki in a new direction. (Compare with irimi.)

UDE-FURI: arm swinging.

UNDO: drill, exercise.

USHIRO-KATA-TORI: an opponent's attack by gripping one's shoulders from behind.

USHIRO-TORI: an opponent's attack by grabbing one in a bear hug from behind.

YOKOMEN-UCHI: an opponent's attack by striking one on the side of the face.

ZEMPO-KAITEN: falling forward.

ZENGO: term indicating forward and backward directions.

KI NO KENKYUKAI H.Q.
101, Ushigome Heim, 2–30 Haramachi, Shinjuku, Tokyo

Tel: 353-3461, 3462

Branches of KI NO KENKYUKAI

Hawaii Ki Society Federation
620 Waipa Lane, Honolulu, HI 96817, U.S.A;   Tel: 808-845-3064

Eastcoast Ki Society Federation
c/o Shizuo Imaizumi
201 East 19th St. Apt. #14J, New York, NY 10003,
U.S.A.   Tel: 212-673-7418

Northwest Ki Society Federation
P.O.Box 02025, Portland, OR 97202, U.S.A.   Tel: 503-223-9124

Midland Ki Society Federation
P.O.Box 818, Boulder, CO 80306, U.S.A.   Tel: 303-442-0505

Northern California Ki Society Federation
1235 De Haro St., San Francisco, CA 94107, U.S.A. Tel: 415-647-8157

Ki No Kenkyukai Italia
Costa de Magnoli 29, 50125 Firenze, Italia   Tel: 055-211962

Ki Federation of Great Britain
c/o Kenneth Williams
Isle Port House , 4 Isle Port Road, Highbridge
Somerset, England

Ki No Kenkyukai Bruxelles
70 Rue Lieutenant Liedel, Bruxelles,   Tel: 02-523-0621
1070, Belgium

Ki-Aikido Dojo Berlin
Hedemannstr. 11, 1000 Berlin 61, West Germany   Tel: 030-251-4696

New Zealand Ki Society
P.O.Box 1140 Auckland, New Zealand

The Shin-Shin Toitsu Aikido School was established in April of 1983 in Tokyo at the KI No Kenkyukai H.Q.

This two year program consists of training of Shin-Shin-Toitsu Aikido techniques and unification of mind and body. Classes are offered in the morning and the evening. Students are to attend class three times a week. Each class is three hours. The first semester is from April to the middle of July and the second semester is from September to the middle of February.

Students from overseas are welcome with the condition that they understand English.

The entrance examination is held in March every year in Tokyo.

KI NO KENKYUKAI H.Q.

101 USHIGOME HEIM, 2-30 HARAMACHI, SHINJUKU-KU, TOKYO

Tel. 03-353-3461, 3462.